HISTORY

THE MISSION OF GOD

AND THE SECRET OF THE GOLDEN THREAD

Can God be trusted?

Learning to love God's Word

History, The Mission of God & The Secret of The Golden Thread
Student Discipleship Guide
Published by Wheaton Press © 2010, 2019
Wheaton, Illinois

www.WheatonPress.com

ISBN-13: 978-1-950258-14-7
ISBN-10: 1-950258-14-9

1. Christian Education – Discipleship 2. Spiritual Formation – Discipleship. 3. Culture & Theology – Education. 4. Nonfiction-Religion and Spirituality-Christian Life. 5. Nonfiction-Spiritual Growth-Christ-centered.

Contact the publisher for discounted copies for partner schools and receive free resources and training for teachers.

Learn more at WheatonPress.com or email WheatonPress@gmail.com

Equipping Students to Reflect
Christ in their circles of influence

	YEAR ONE	YEAR TWO	YEAR THREE
Growth Emphasis	An Emphasis on Belonging	An Emphasis on Identity	An Emphasis on Purpose
Essential Questions	1. How do I understand God's Word? 2. How do I love God's Word?	3. How do I approach God? 4. How do I relate to God, myself and others?	5. How do I make sense of the world? 6. Who will I follow?
Essential Outcomes	Understand and articulate the Christ-centered Narrative	Develop authentic Christ-centered relationships	Develop a clear Christ-centered personal mission
Courses	HiStory, The Mission of God and the secret of the Golden Thread True Hero	The X things God wants you to know about Himself ID: Learning to relate to God, myself and others	TALMIDIM; the path of the disciple Witness & Worldview
Leadership Pipeline	D Groups	Mentor Project	The Glory Project
Answering the Essential Questions	**Belonging**: Where do I fit?	**Identity**: Who am I?	Purpose: What will I do?

Essential Questions

1 How do I understand and love God & His Word?

2 How will I respond and find my place in His story?

Stops on the Journey

1 Plot

2 Prologue

3 Patriarchs

4 Passover

5 Pillar

6 Promised

7 Proximity

Course Description

This course invites students on a global journey to examine the historicity and the plot of the greatest story ever told. Students will be challenged to objectively investigate four of the significant motifs throughout the plot of the Hebrew Bible.

This is not a survey course but an introduction to a relational, missional God who created us with purpose and invites us to know Him, and not merely about Him. Students will be invited to consider a personal relationship and to practice a daily awareness in their approach and response to the God of the Bible.

Students will interact with the disciplines of language, literary analysis, archeology, geography, and history while having the opportunity for a personal application and personal contribution. Students will produce several unique and distinct projects to demonstrate understanding and provide opportunities to practice creativity while building relational and communication skills,

Remember your Creator in the days of your youth before the days of trouble come...
Ecclesiastes 12:1

Course Overview

The Mission of God and the Secret of the Golden Thread invites students on a global journey to evaluate the trustworthiness of the Bible and the claims that it makes. Throughout the journey, students will examine the plot and four significant motifs within the story of Scripture to uncover the secret of the Golden thread and how it applies to their lives.

Learning Outcomes

A Students will examine the question of purpose and begin the process of understanding their unique story and God's individual purpose for their lives in light of His eternal mission.

B Students will analyze the doctrine of the Imago Dei as it impacts their identity and how they relate to God and others.

C Students will identify and examine main events and developments within the overall story of the Bible and be able to connect characters, geography, and motifs into the whole historical plotline.

D Students will begin to lay the foundation for understanding the concepts of worldview and integration as discipleship by examining the theme of the Kingdom and glory of God that is introduced in Genesis 1 and culminates in Revelation 22.

E Students will be challenged to exercise personal creativity through project-based learning assessments designed to invite the communication of understanding and application.

F Students will demonstrate an understanding of the concepts they have learned by applying them through a cross-disciplinary project that is designed, assembled, developed, and constructed by their class.

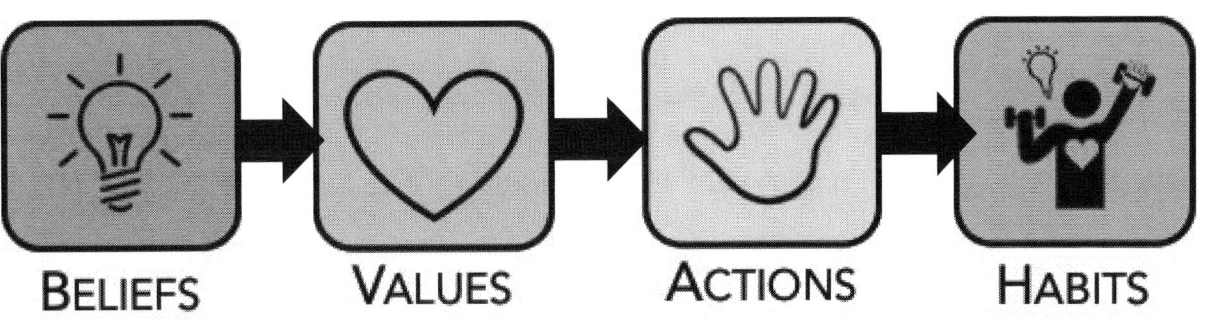

Course Overview

Unit 1. Plot

1. What is the learning goal for this course?
2. What can I expect from this course?
3. What will my personal contribution be?
4. What is the difference between a story and a plot?
5. What is a motif?
6. What is the Bible?
7. What is the plot of the Bible?

Unit 2. Prologue

1. What is the Imago Dei?
2. What is the Missio Dei?
3. What was life like in the Garden?
4. What is temptation? What is sin?
5. How do I understand God's grace?
6. What is the difference between religion and true worship?
7. Can God be trusted?
8. How will I demonstrate learning in a creative and meaningful way?

Unit 3. Patriarchs

1. Why does God choose Abram?
2. What happens when I fail to trust God?
3. Why does God choose Jacob the deceiver?
4. How do I respond when I'm tempted?
5. Why do bad things happen in spite of right choices?
6. Can God be trusted?
7. How do I forgive?
8. How will I demonstrate learning in a creative and meaningful way?

Unit 4. Passover

1. How does God use Egypt to fulfill His mission?
2. Who is Moses?
3. How does God reveal Himself to His people?
4. How does God reveal Himself to the world?
5. What is The Passover?
6. Can God be trusted?
7. How will I demonstrate learning in a creative and meaningful way?

Unit 5. Pillar

1. Is God efficient?
2. How does God reveal Himself through The Law?
3. How does God reveal Himself through The Festivals and Feasts?
4. How does God reveal Himself through the Tabernacle?
5. What is faith in the face of fear?
6. Can God be trusted in the wilderness?
7. How will I communicate learning in a creative and meaningful way?

Unit 6. Promised

1. How does God keep His promise and advance His mission through the land of Israel?
2. What is the lesson from the time of the judges?
3. What can I learn from the lives of Samuel & Saul?
4. Why should I remember my Creator in the days of my youth? (The childhood of David)
5. Can I recover from failure?
6. What can I learn from "*the fifth gospel*?"
7. What is significant about Sukkot and Solomon's Temple?

Unit 7. Proximity

1. Why does proximity matter and how do I apply the principles of proximity to my life?
2. What can I learn from the division and exile of Israel?
3. Can God be trusted?
4. How will I celebrate and communicate learning?

HISTORY

THE MISSION OF GOD

AND THE SECRET OF THE GOLDEN THREAD

plot

Can God be trusted?

Learning to love God's Word

And you shall make a veil of blue and purple and scarlet yarns and fine twined linen.

Exodus 26:31

What is the learning goal for History, The Mission of God & The Secret of the Golden Thread?

What does it mean when we say that the Bible is not anti-atheism, it is anti-idolatry?

WORD

What is the Bible?

Did you know that the Bible is the best-selling (and most shoplifted) book in the history of the world?

It was written over a period of 1,500 years, by over 40 different authors, and across 3 different continents (Africa, Asia, and Europe).

It was originally written in three different languages (Aramaic, Hebrew, and Greek) and by the year 500 AD, it was translated into over 600 languages.

It has 66 books that consist of 39 in the Hebrew Old Testament and 27 in the Greek New Testament.

Yet within all of those differences, time, authors, languages, it speaks with internal consistency as on single unified book that tells on a single unified story.

His Story

The Bible is the eternal story of God. It is a historical book that accurately reveals what happened in real-time in real places that you and I can visit for ourselves.

The Bible is also a prophetic book.

A quarter of the Bible was prophetic at the time that it was written and it has accurately seen hundreds and hundreds of often precise prophecies fulfilled time and again.

But one interesting thing that many people do not realize is the Bible does not prove the existence of God.

In fact, the Bible does not even attempt to prove the existence of God.

Instead, the Bible assumes the existence of God. From the very first words of the Bible, the presumption is made that "in the beginning God..."

In light of that, it is important to understand that the Bible is not "anti-atheism," instead, it is better for us to realize that the Bible is "anti-idolatry."

It is with this in mind that you are invited to study the plot, story, and themes of the Hebrew Old Testament during this course.

Day or Night at the Museum

Congratulations!

Your class has been asked by the Head of School to create a museum to teach younger students and members of the community about the overall purpose and plotline of the Bible.

Included in the museum will be artifacts representing each of the main stages of the Old Testament plot as well as displays that connect to archeology, geography, languages, apologetics, art and bibliology.

The museum is not intended to present a survey of the storyline of the Hebrew Old Testament but an introduction to a relational, missional God who gives us purpose and invites us to know Him and not merely to know about Him.

People who attend the museum should leave understanding that the God of the Bible invites us into a personal relationship that is not based on religious activity or appeasement.

The Museum experience should provide participants an invitation to learn how to approach the relational, missional God of the Bible who invites us to understand and participate in His mission, His promise and His Kingdom.

The Museum will have 7 display areas

1. Lobby
2. Prologue
3. Patriarchs
4. Passover
5. Pillars
6. Promised Land
7. Proximity

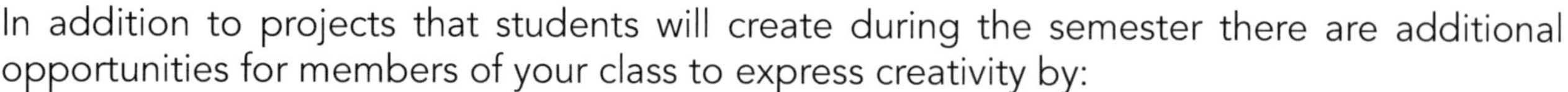
In addition to projects that students will create during the semester there are additional opportunities for members of your class to express creativity by:

- Making costumes
- Preparing a food from a different culture
- Creating artwork from different culture
- Creating marketing for social media, school publications and communication to other classes within the school.
- Creating a logo and branding for your museum.
- You are encouraged to be creative in accomplishing your mission.
- You are encouraged to learn from and share ideas with a global community of students who are working on the same project in their local community around the world.

Museum Employee Identification and Biography Project

There are three parts to this project.

Part I. Personal Timeline

You will create a personal timeline of your life. Start by identifying significant events in your life like when and where were you born, if you have you moved, changed houses or schools, or if there have been additions to your family since you have been born? Identify other fun activities, memories, achievements, or accomplishments. Have their been particular family vacations or memories that you have enjoyed?

Write each event on a card and then paste or tape the cards in order along a timeline on a large sheet of paper. Then personalize your timeline with illustrations and pictures.

You are encouraged to be as creative as you want.

Your timeline should reflect your personality.

Part II. Employee Bio

Once you have completed your timeline, it is time to write your biography for your museum employee biography. At the end of the semester, these biographies will be displayed near the entrance to the museum to help those in attendance get to know you better. Use the template located in your student guide and the information from your personal timeline to write your biography.

Part III. Employee Picture

You need to have your picture taken for your ID badge. Your picture should reflect your personality and your occupation of choice within the museum?

You are encouraged to use props or costumes for your picture. Consider being a scientist, archeologist, explorer, museum curator, food service, or even an employee in the museum gift shop. The choice is yours.

Props can include but are not limited to: hats, mustaches on a stick, approved signs to hold.

Group photos, as well as individual photos, are also encouraged.

Five essential elements of a story

Characters. The individuals that the story is about. There should be enough detailed description that the reader can visualize each person. Every story should have a main character.

Setting. The location of the action. The environment or surroundings should be described in detail so that the reader feels that they can picture the scene.

Plot. The actual story upon which the book is based. A plot should have a clear beginning, middle, and end.

Conflict. Every story has a conflict to solve. The plot is centered on this conflict and the ways in which the characters attempt to resolve the problem.

Resolution. The solutions to the problem. It is important that the resolution fit the rest of the story in tone and creativity and solve all the parts of the conflict.

Six essential elements of a plot

Exposition. What information does the writer give you at the beginning of the story? How are the setting and the characters established? (conflict, character, setting).

Rising Action. What events in the rising action drew you in the most as a reader? The character attempts to solve the problem but fails.

Conflict. What types of conflict are present in the story? How did you identify them?

Climax. This is often considered the most exciting or suspenseful part of the story. The turning point; the point of greatest suspense or action.

Falling Action. In what way is the action in this part of the story different from the first part? Action and events that occur after the climax.

Resolution. How does this part of the story make you feel? The end of the story is where the conflicts or problems are solved.

Who am I?

Museum Employee Character Study

Museum Group Marketing Project

Welcome to your start-up museum! Since you are a start-up, you need to think about all of the things that a start-up museum needs.

- A name – What will you name your museum?
- A logo – Do you need to have a logo? How will you decide which one is the best fit?
- A brand – Do you have specific colors or a particular theme that you are trying to have?
- Marketing – Do you want to make posters? Should they be digital or drawn by hand?
- Invitations – Do you want to invite other classes or members of your families?
- What method of communication to you want to use to represent your museum?

Part I. Research

- It's time to research some of the best museums in the world that display artifacts from the Bible. There are museums in London, Paris, Berlin, Greece, Jerusalem, and Chicago that you will want to visit. Since plane fare is expensive (and was not figured into your tuition) we will need to visit each of these museums virtually.
- You are encouraged to explore each of the museums. Take notes of what you discover. Not only in the artifacts and what is being displayed but how they are being displayed. You will find that some are quite plain, while others are more visually interesting. Some have specific activities for students. Since your museum might be open to the younger classes, are there things that you should consider creating?
- Take notes and consider how you want to design the museum that your class will create.
- The first stop is London, England, and a trip to the World Renown British Museum.
- Additional stops will include The Louvre in Paris, The Shrine of the Book in Jerusalem (museum for The Dead Sea Scrolls),and finally the Oriental Museum in Chicago.

The British Museum

15 APR 18
ENGLAND
LONDON
VISIT PASS

The British Museum with Google
https://www.britishmuseum.org/with_google.aspx

The British Museum
https://www.britishmuseum.org

The British Museum for schools
https://www.britishmuseum.org/learning/schools_and_teachers.aspx

The British Museum – Bust of Ramessess II
http://www.teachinghistory100.org/objects/bust_of_ramesses_ii

MUSÉE DU LOUVRE

https://www.youtube.com/watch?v=vmKeRxv-xwM

https://www.youvisit.com/louvremuseum

http://stockholm360.net/index.php

https://oi.uchicago.edu/virtualtour

https://www.imj.org.il/en/wings/shrine-book/model-jerusalem-second-temple-period

The Shrine of the Book
https://www.imj.org.il/en/collection-galleries

Museum Group Marketing Project

Part II. Design Phase

Now that you have researched various museums you need to begin to design your own. At the end of the allotted time you will need to have decided upon a name, a logo, and the layout of the museum.

To plan for the layout you will want to learn from your teacher or your administration the space they are giving you for your museum. Will you be using the school foyer? Will you be in the gym or multi-purpose room? Or will there be other space.

Once you know the space you have been given you will want to mark out the areas. Perhaps you will want to use masking tape to mark the floor. Or you may have students stand in different places to illustrate different rooms or areas.

At the end you will want to make drawings or take pictures so that you know where and how you will set up the museum at the end of the semester.

•Where will you have people enter?

•What path will they follow?

Here are some important things about your museum to know.

Area 1. Entrance. Your museum will have an entrance that will display your ID badges and your biographies.

Area 2. Prologue. This area will display dioramas illustrating the first 11 chapters of the book of Genesis.

Area 3. Patriarchs. This area will display busts (heads) of the Patriarchs and Matriarchs of the nation of Israel. Near each of the busts will be a written character analysis.

Area 4. Passover. This area will include old fashioned television documentaries explaining Israel's time in Egypt, the plagues, The Passover and how God delivered His people.

Area 5. Pillar. This area will include models of the Tabernacle.

Area 6. Promised Land. This area will include salt dough maps of the nation of Israel, and surrounding nations.

Area 7. Proximity. This area will host a Purim spiel. A Purim spiel is a humorous, play or "readers theatre" that retells the historical events of Purim as recorded in the book of Esther.

Why did God give us the Bible?

What I think | **What my partner thinks**

What God says

1. So that we would know ________________

What does this mean and why does it matter?

"I revealed myself to those who did not ask for me; I was found by those who did not seek me.

To a nation that did not call on my name, I said, 'Here am I, here am I.' All day long I have held out my hands..."

Isaiah 65:1-2a

2. So that we would know ________________

What does this mean and why does it matter?

God has now revealed to us his mysterious will regarding Christ—which is to fulfill his own good plan. And this is the plan: At the right time he will bring everything together under the authority of Christ—everything in heaven and on earth.

Ephesians 1:9-10

3. So that we would know ________________

What does this mean and why does it matter?

The Lord has made his salvation known and revealed his righteousness to every nation! He remembered his promise to love and be faithful to Israel. The ends of the earth have seen the victory of our God.

Psalm 98:2

How does the Bible invite me to use it to approach God?

1. I am invited to approach God's word as a _______________ because . . .

> "Your word is a lamp to my feet and a light to my path."
> Psalm 119:105

2. I am invited to approach God's word with a desire to be _______________ because . . .

> "Do not merely listen to the word, and so deceive yourselves. Do what it says."
> James 1:22

3. I am invited to approach God's word with an attitude of _______________ because . . .

> Shout for joy to the Lord, all the earth. [2] Worship the Lord with gladness; come before him with joyful songs.
>
> [3] Know that the Lord is God. It is he who made us, and we are his; we are his people, the sheep of his pasture.
>
> [4] Enter his gates with thanksgiving and his courts with praise; give thanks to him and praise his name.
>
> [5] For the Lord is good and his love endures forever; his faithfulness continues through all generations.
>
> Psalm 100

How are the books of the Hebrew Bible organized?

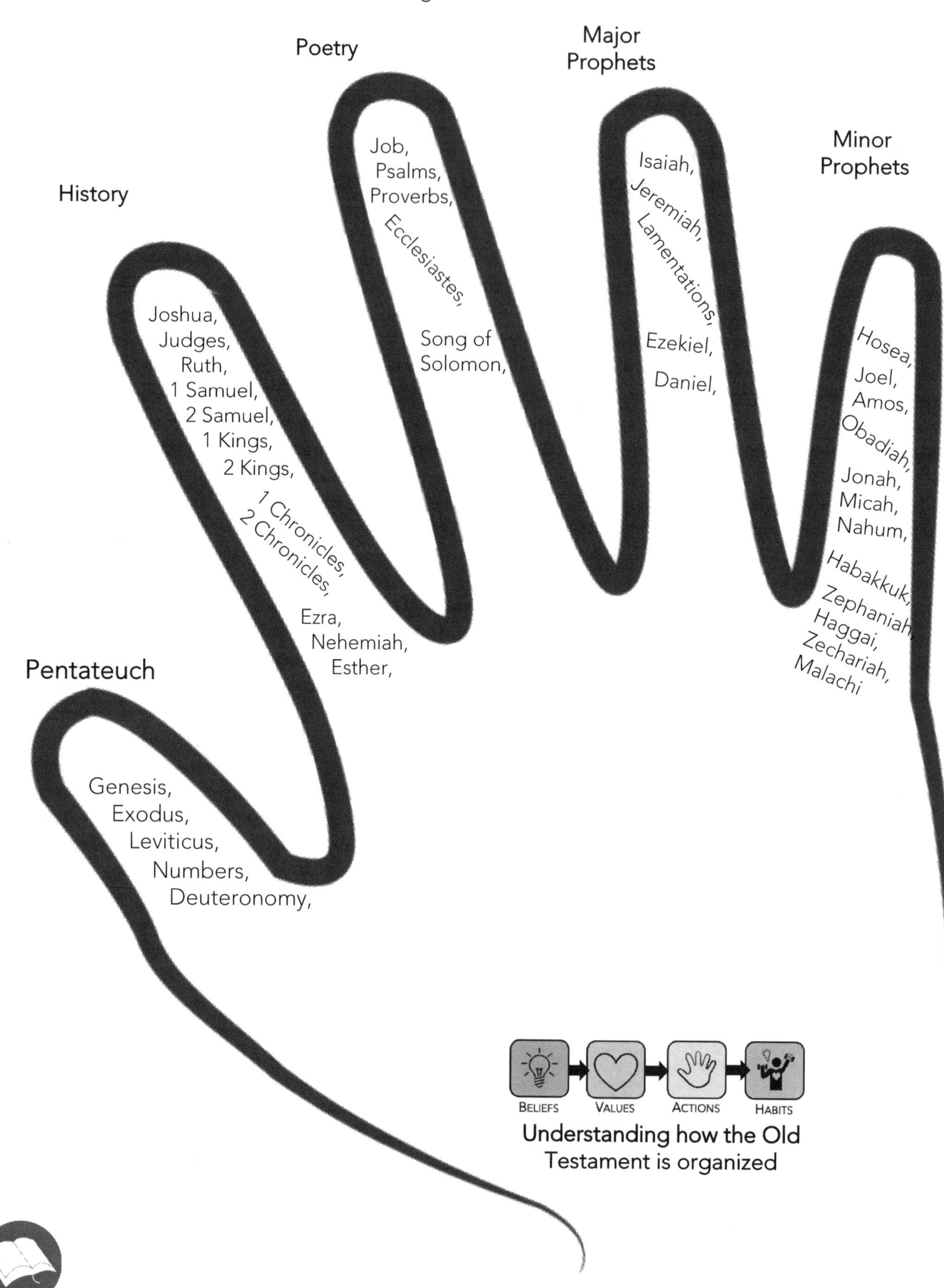

What is the setting?

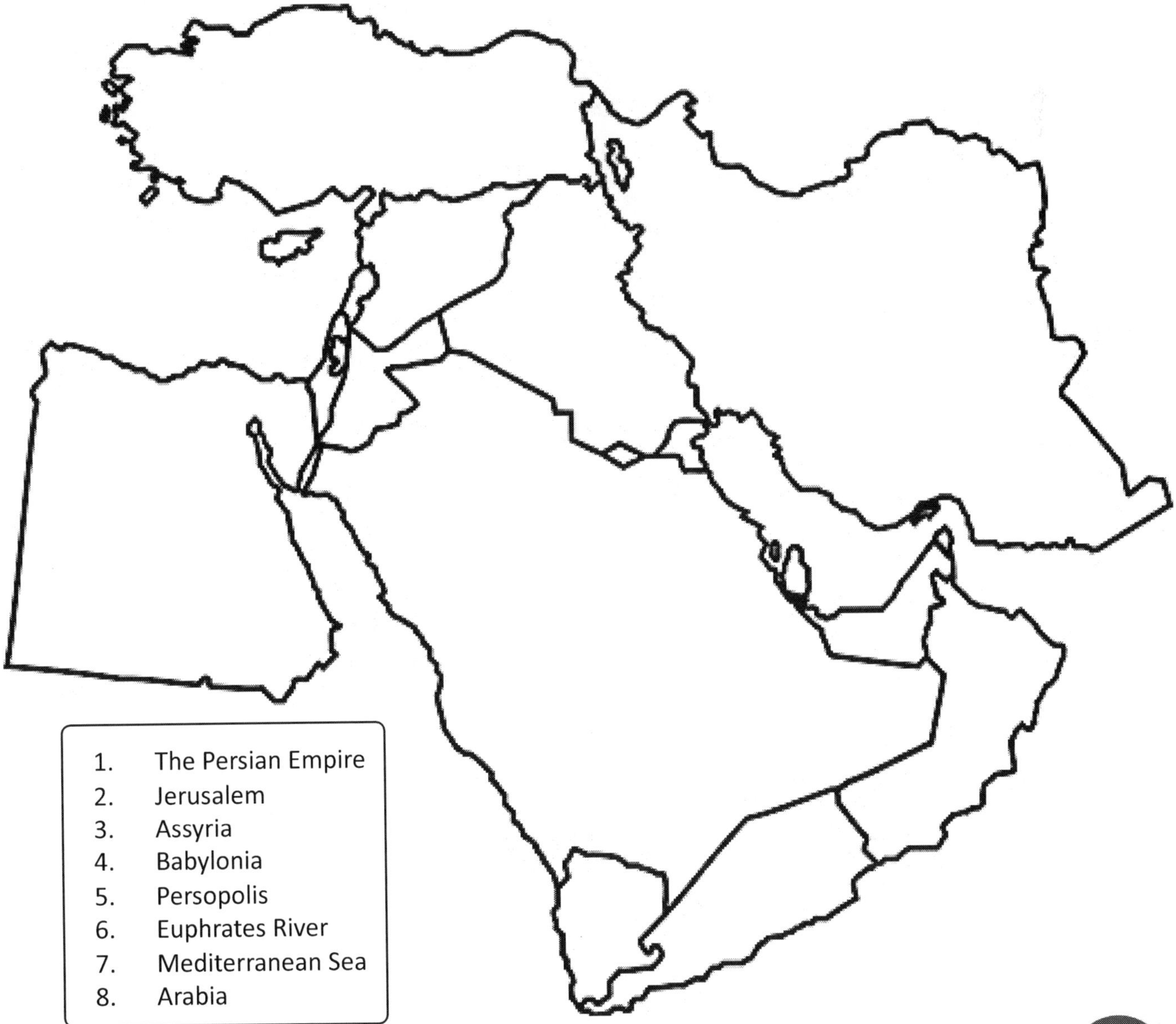

1. The Persian Empire
2. Jerusalem
3. Assyria
4. Babylonia
5. Persopolis
6. Euphrates River
7. Mediterranean Sea
8. Arabia

THE BLUE THREAD

PROLOGUE

EDEN · ADAM · CAIN · NOAH · NATIONS · BABEL

PATRIARCH

ABRAHAM · ISAAC · JACOB · JOSEPH

PASSOVER

JOSEPH · MOSES · PLAGUES · PASSOVER

PILLAR

PILLAR · SINAI · TABERNACLE · THE ARK · FESTIVALS

PROMISED

JOSHUA · DAVID · THE TEMPLE

PROXIMITY

DIVISION/EXILE · RETURN

And you shall make a veil of blue and purple and scarlet yarns and fine twined linen. Exodus 26:31

WHAT ARE SOME MAJOR MILESTONES IN THE OLD TESTAMENT PLOTLINE?

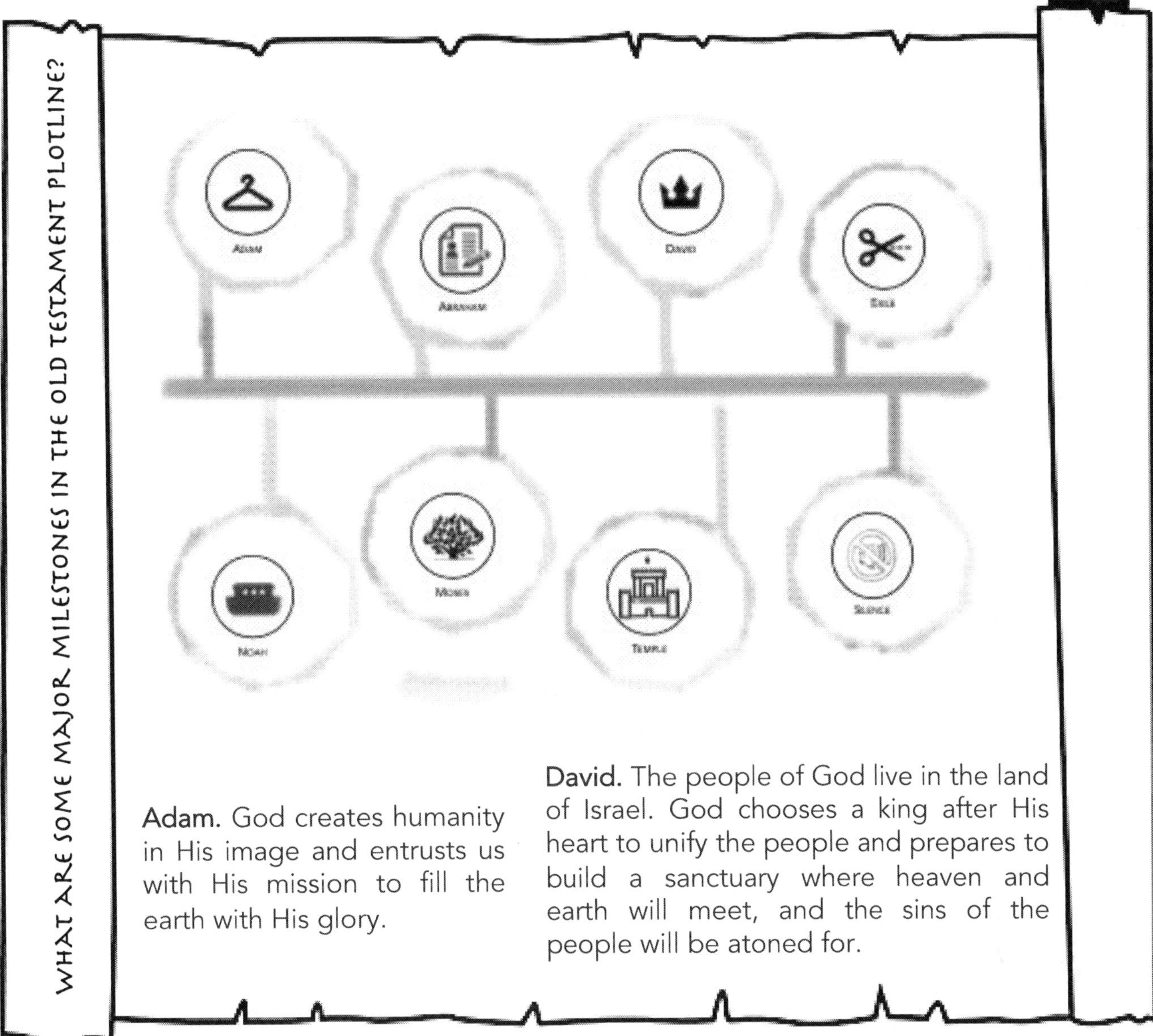

Adam. God creates humanity in His image and entrusts us with His mission to fill the earth with His glory.

David. The people of God live in the land of Israel. God chooses a king after His heart to unify the people and prepares to build a sanctuary where heaven and earth will meet, and the sins of the people will be atoned for.

Noah. The sin of mankind increases, and we fill the earth with evil. God demonstrates His perfect justice by flooding the earth to cleanse it and His perfect grace by providing an ark to preserve His purpose and His promise.

Abraham. God chooses Abram and promises to fulfill His purpose to fill the earth with His glory through his family.

Moses. The descendants of Abraham become enslaved in Egypt. God chooses a leader to speak His words and lead His people from slavery to the land He promised them.

Temple. God directs Solomon to build a sanctuary where He will dwell among His people. Through this sacred space, the people of God and the nations of the world will see His glory, grace, and truth.

Exile. The people of God rebel and fail to follow His commands. Their hearts stray from His dwelling place, and they are removed from the land that He promised to them. God sends prophets to call their hearts back to Him, remind them of His love and refocus them toward a promised Messiah who will deliver them.

Silence. A remnant remains faithful to God, and after some time, a new generation returns and awaits the promised deliverer with anticipation and expectation.

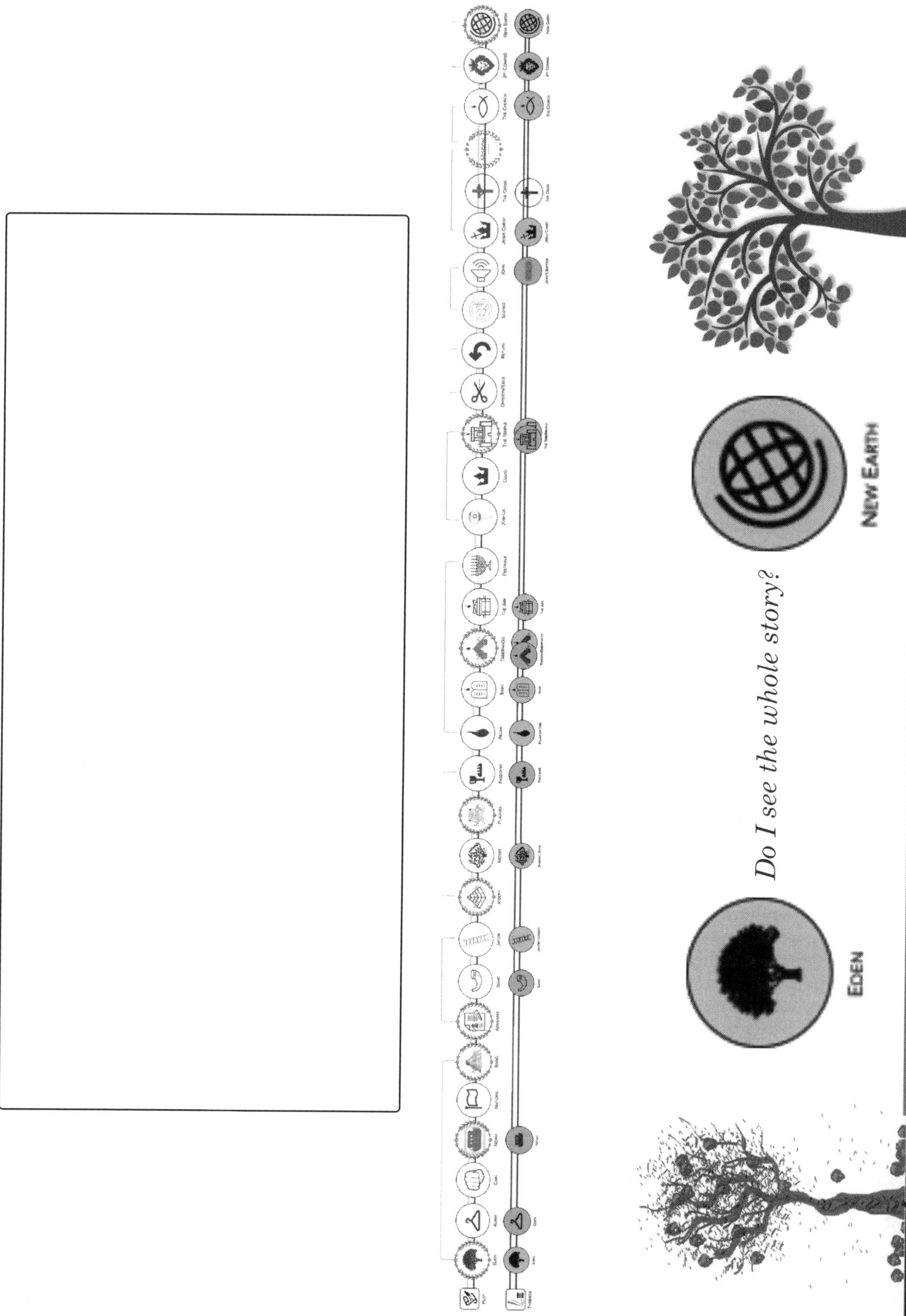
Do I see the whole story?
Eden
New Earth
And you shall make a veil of blue and purple and scarlet yarns and fine twined linen. Exodus 26:31

Praise his glorious name forever! Let the whole earth be filled with his glory. Amen and amen! Psalm 72:19

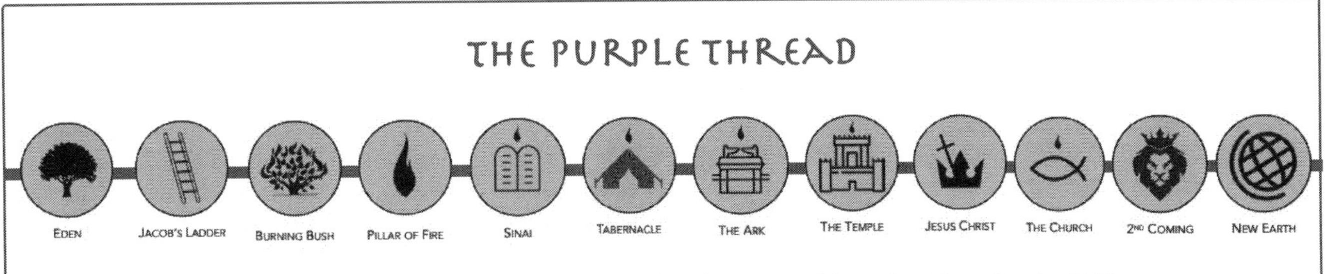

And you shall make a veil of blue and purple and scarlet yarns and fine twined linen. Exodus 26:31

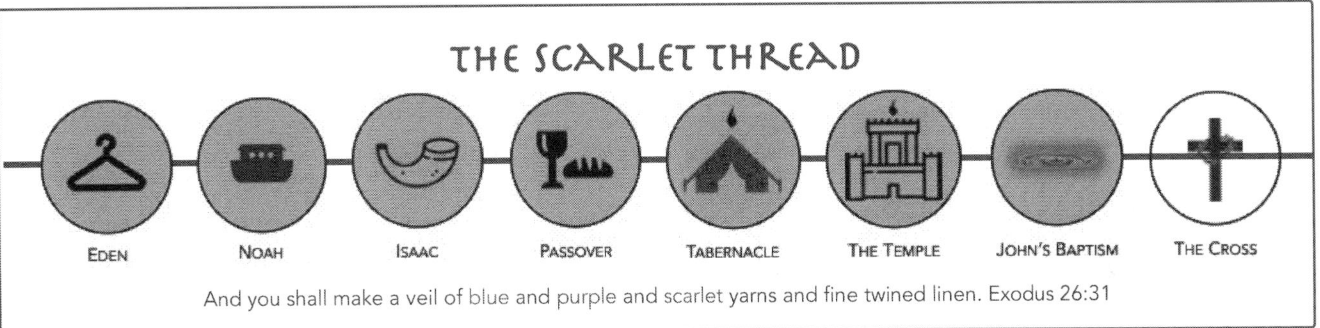

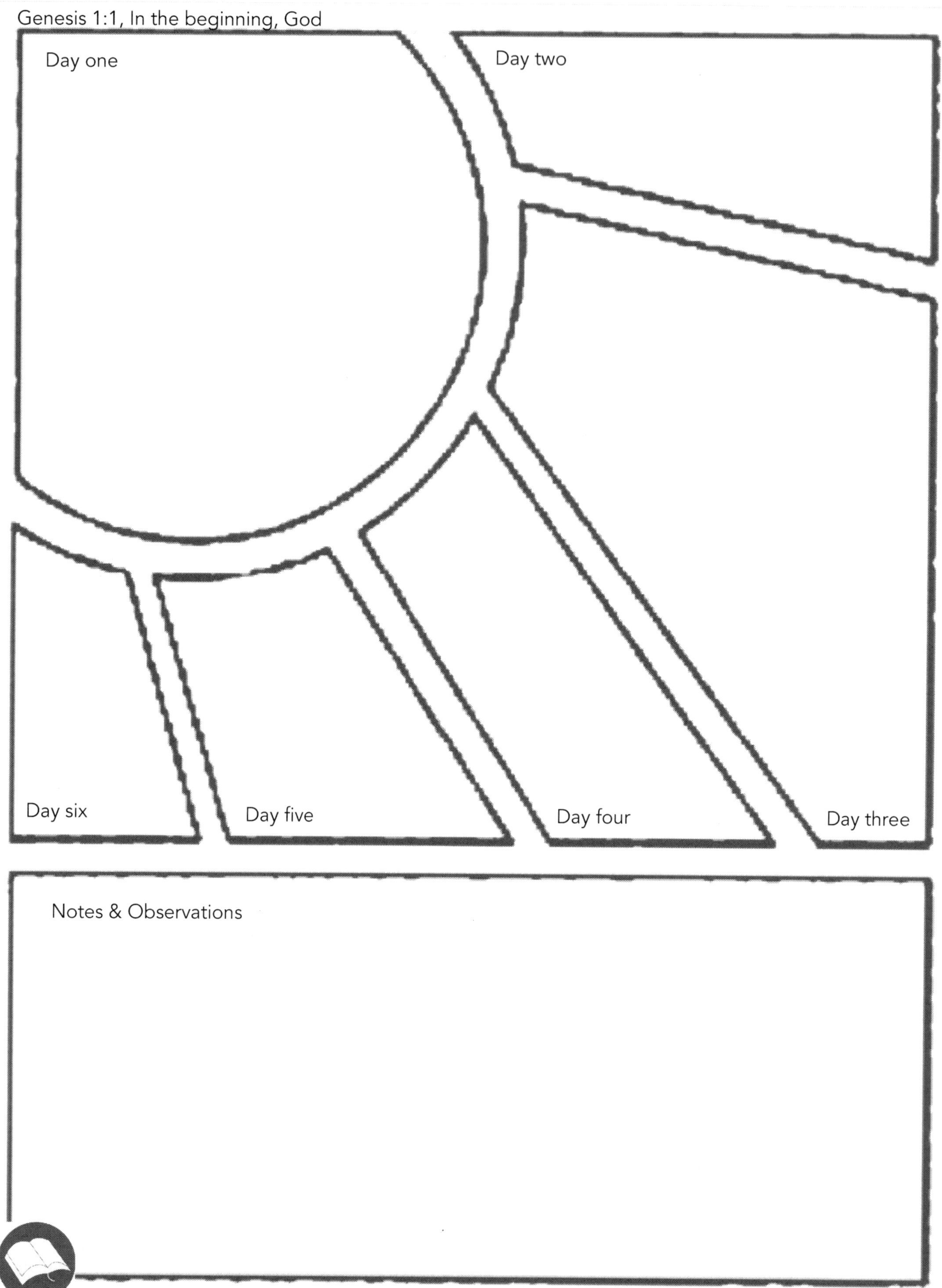
Genesis 1:1, In the beginning, God
Day one
Day two
Day three
Day four
Day five
Day six
Notes & Observations

Plot. How does the story end?

REVELATION 7:7-12

After this I looked, and there before me was a great multitude that no one could count, from every nation, tribe, people and language, standing before the throne and before the Lamb. They were wearing white robes and were holding palm branches in their hands. 10 And they cried out in a loud voice:

"Salvation belongs to our God, who sits on the throne, and to the Lamb."11 All the angels were standing around the throne and around the elders and the four living creatures. They fell down on their faces before the throne and worshiped God, 12 saying: "Amen! Praise and glory and wisdom and thanks and honorand power and strength be to our God for ever and ever. Amen!"

REVELATION 7:7-12

REVELATION 21: 1-6,10

A NEW HEAVEN AND A NEW EARTH

21 Then I saw "a new heaven and a new earth," for the first heaven and the first earth had passed away, and there was no longer any sea. 2 I saw the Holy City, the new Jerusalem, coming down out of heaven from God, prepared as a bride beautifully dressed for her husband. 3 And I heard a loud voice from the throne saying, "Look! God's dwelling place is now among the people, and he will dwell with them. They will be his people, and God himself will be with them and be their God. 4 'He will wipe every tear from their eyes. There will be no more death' or mourning or crying or pain, for the old order of things has passed away."
5 He who was seated on the throne said, "I am making everything new!" Then he said, "Write this down, for these words are trustworthy and true."
6 He said to me: "It is done. I am the Alpha and the Omega, the Beginning and the End... "Come, I will show you the bride, the wife of the Lamb."
10 And he carried me away in the Spirit to a mountain great and high, and showed me the Holy City, Jerusalem, coming down out of heaven from God.

11 It shone with the glory of God, and its brilliance was like that of a very precious jewel, like a jasper, clear as crystal. 12 It had a great, high wall with twelve gates, and with twelve angels at the gates. On the gates were written the names of the twelve tribes of Israel. 13 There were three gates on the east, three on the north, three on the south and three on the west. 14 The wall of the city had twelve foundations, and on them were the names of the twelve apostles of the Lamb...

The great street of the city was of gold, as pure as transparent glass.
22 I did not see a temple in the city, because the Lord God Almighty and the Lamb are its temple. 23 The city does not need the sun or the moon to shine on it, for the glory of God gives it light, and the Lamb is its lamp. 24 The nations will walk by its light, and the kings of the earth will bring their splendor into it. 25 On no day will its gates ever be shut, for there will be no night there. 26 The glory and honor of the nations will be brought into it. 27 Nothing impure will ever enter it, nor will anyone who does what is shameful or deceitful, but only those whose names are written in the Lamb's book of life.

REVELATION 21:11-14, 22-27

Plot. The Elements of the story

Setting:
Where:

When:

Major Characters:

Minor Characters:

Plot/Problem:

Event 1:

Event 2:

Event 3:

Outcome:

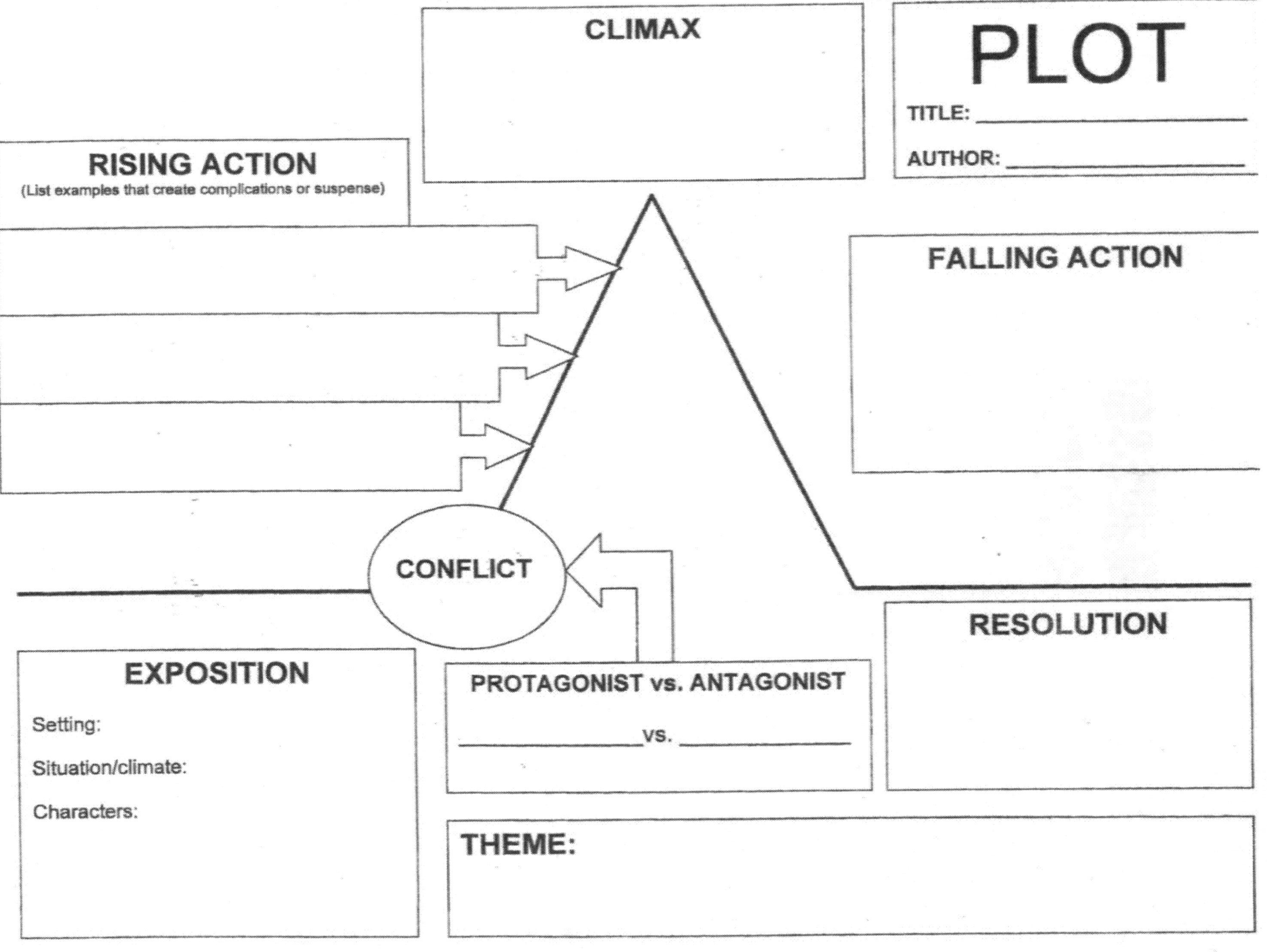
PLOT
TITLE:
AUTHOR:
CLIMAX
RISING ACTION
(List examples that create complications or suspense)
FALLING ACTION
CONFLICT
RESOLUTION
EXPOSITION
Setting:
Situation/climate:
Characters:
PROTAGONIST vs. ANTAGONIST
vs.
THEME:

Assessment & Project

Collaboration Rubric				
	Below Standard	Approaching Standard	At Standard	Above Standard
Takes Personal Responsibility for Learning and Contributing to the Learning Process	Not prepared, informed or ready to contribute to the team. Does not utilize technology as agreed upon. Does not participate in project tasks. Does not listen to or use feedback to improve work	Usually prepared, and ready to work with team. Does not utilize technology according to agreed upon standards with consistency. Needs reminding or prompting to complete tasks. Uses some feedback and complete most tasks	Prepared and ready to work. Well informed and cites evidence that encourages learning among other team members. Consistently uses technology as agree upon. Self motivated and does not need to be reminded to complete tasks. Completes tasks on time. Evaluates and uses feedback to improve work.	
Contribution to the Team	Does not help the team to solve problems; may be the source of problems for the team. Does not ask probing questions, express ideas, or elaborate in response to questions or discussions. Does not offer help. Does not provide useful feedback	Cooperates but does not active participant. Asks probing questions occasionally, expresses an idea in responses to discussions. Sometimes offers help. Sometimes provides feedback but it may not always be helpful.	Helps the team to solve problems and manage conflict. Clearly expresses ideas, asks probing questions, listens to others and solicits feedback from quiet team members to ensure that all perspectives are shared and heard. Provides useful feedback Identifies opportunities to Appropriately helps others.	
Relationships and Respect	Impolite or unkind to team members (may interrupt, ignore, talk over or use hurtful words or body language). Does not listen or respect other perspectives	Usually polite and kind to team members. Usually listens and respects team members. Disagrees with content, perspectives and opinions without attacking the person.	Polite and kind to team members. Listens to, acknowledges and respects other team members. Disagrees with content and builds community by affirming the person	

Student Study Guide

- The Bible does not prove the existence of God.
- The Bible Presumes the Existence of God.
- The Bible is a historical book.
- The Bible is God's special method of revealing Himself to us.
- The Bible was written in Africa, Asia, and Europe.
- The Bible was written by over 40 authors.
- The Bible was written in three languages (Aramaic, Hebrew, Greek).
- The Bible has 66 books.
- The Old Testament has 39 books.
- The New Testament has 27 books.
- The Old Testament has 5 main categories (Pentateuch, History, Poetry, Major Prophets, Minor Prophets).
- The Bible is one unified book made up of two testaments.
- What Old Testament name is the name Jesus derived from?
- What does the name Jesus mean?

HISTORY
THE MISSION OF GOD
AND THE SECRET OF THE GOLDEN THREAD

prologue
Can God be trusted?
Learning to love God's Word

So God created mankind in His own *image*, in the *image* of God He created them; male and female He created them. God blessed them and said to them,

"Be fruitful and increase in number; fill the earth and subdue it."

Genesis 1:27-28

What is the learning goal for Prologue?

A prologue is used to give readers extra information that advances the plot. It is included in the front for a good reason! Authors use them for various purposes, including: Giving background information about the story, introducing us to the main characters, helping us understand the setting, and introducing the conflict that will become central to the story.

PLOT

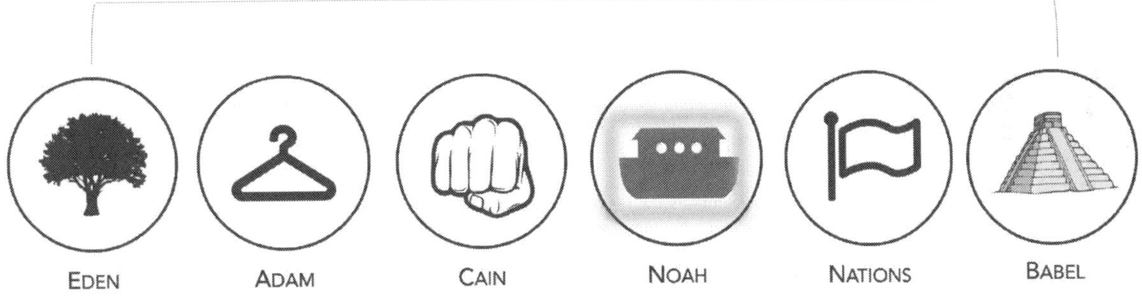

The word Genesis means beginnings.

In the first three chapters of Genesis, God reveals to us the beginnings of several **plot threads** that are woven throughout the rest of the **narrative** of the Bible.

In Genesis, we learn that God created humanity in His image and that He entrusts us with His mission to fill the earth with His glory.

We are also introduced to the conflict.

It turns out that humanity desires to reflect our own glory. So instead of enjoying a perfect relationship with God and life as it was intended to be lived, humans choose to place their will above God's.

God had instructed Adam and Eve that if they were to rebel and disobey Him that it would result in death, but God demonstrates **forbearance** and implements a process to cover our shame and reconnect us with Himself and His purpose.

But there is a catch.

It turns out that humans like to rebel against God, and in spite of the consequences, it does not take long before we have filled the earth with everything except the glory of God.

And so begins the rising action. The question becomes whether or not the earth will be filled with the glory of God before the story ends.

Prologue; The story begins

Setting:
Where:

When:

Major Characters:

Minor Characters:

Plot/Problem:

Event 1:

Event 2:

Event 3:

Outcome:

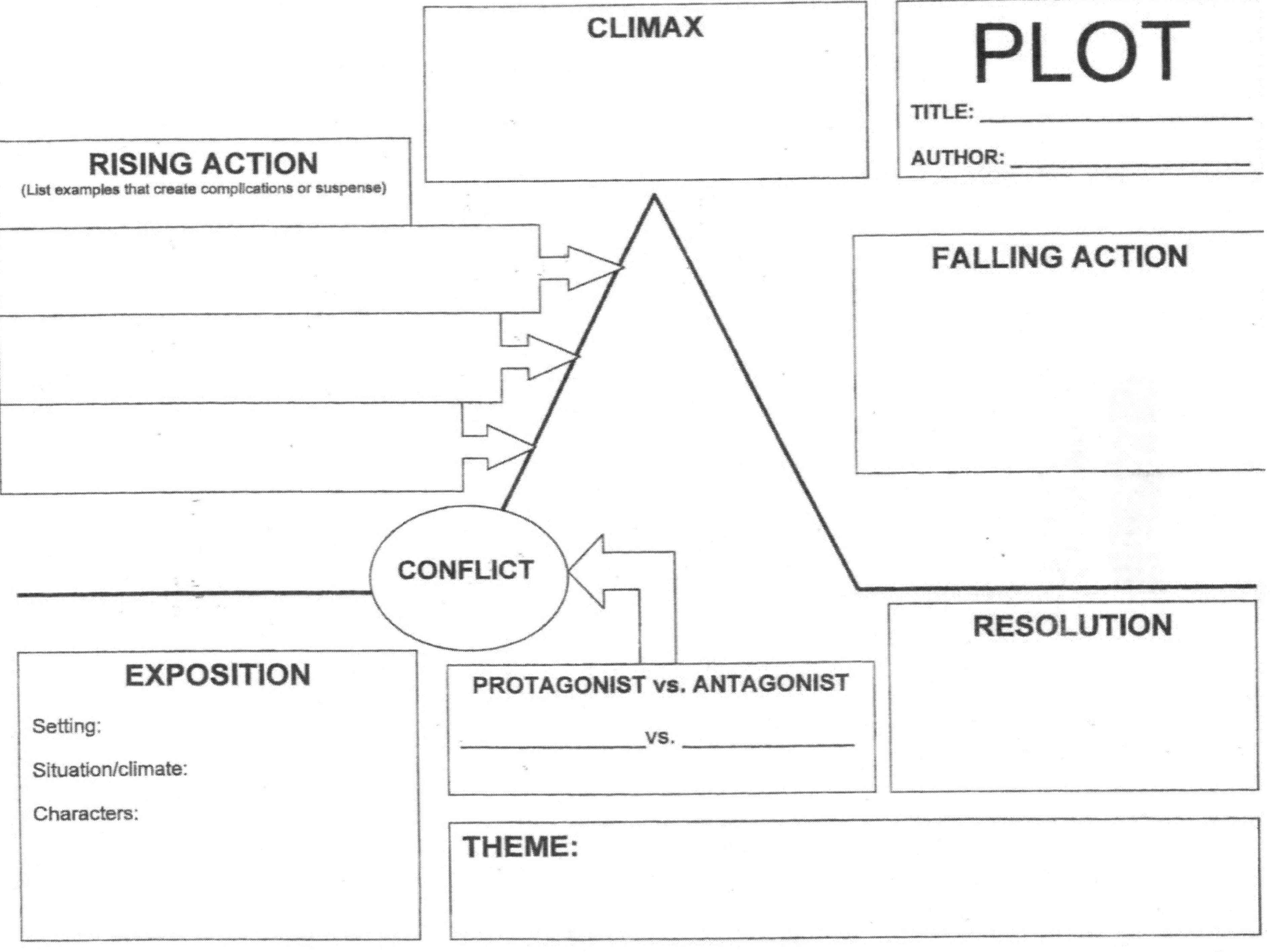
CLIMAX
PLOT
TITLE:
AUTHOR:
RISING ACTION
(List examples that create complications or suspense)
FALLING ACTION
CONFLICT
RESOLUTION
EXPOSITION
Setting:
Situation/climate:
Characters:
PROTAGONIST vs. ANTAGONIST
vs.
THEME:

What is the Imago Dei?

What makes humans unique?

Genesis reveals that in the beginning, God made man and woman in his image. He breathed his life into their nostrils, and we became living beings.

The term *Imago Dei* is a Latin phrase which means "Image of God."

All humans inherit the image of God inside of us, but it is not perfect anymore because of the impact and separation caused by sin.

Then God said, "Let us make mankind in our image, in our likeness, so that they may rule over the fish in the sea and the birds in the sky, over the livestock and all the wild animals, and over all the creatures that move along the ground."
Genesis 1:26

If the Imago Dei is true, then how should it impact the way that I relate to myself?

If the Imago Dei is true, then how should it impact the way that I relate to others?

So God created mankind in his own image, in the image of God he created them; male and female he created them. Genesis 1:27

How does the Imago Dei equip me to make sense of the world I live in?

Assignment. What are some of the different areas that people relate to themselves and others that are impacted by a proper understanding and application of the Imago Dei?

What do I think?

Pair & Share One

Pair & Share Two

How should this impact my life? *(head, hearts, hands, habits)*

BELIEFS

VALUES

ACTIONS

HABITS

What is the Missio Dei?

What is the mission that God gave to Adam & Eve?

Genesis reveals that God not only made humanity in His image but that He shared with them a precise instruction that He would repeat to others throughout the rest of the plot of the Bible.

A word used to describe the type of instruction that God gave to Adam and Eve is the word "mandate." A mandate is an official order or a commission to do something. By giving Adam His mandate, God was inviting Him (and eventually us) to share His mission with Him (to co-mission).

Another aspect of a mandate is that a mandate carries the concept of authority. In other words, a person who receives a mandate to do something must also be given the authority to accomplish the mission or the goal.

The concept of a being given a mandate with authority to co-mission or to share in God's mission can be observed in Genesis and then seen as it is developed throughout Scripture through what is called *Missio Dei.*

The term ***Missio Dei*** is a Latin phrase which means "Mission of God" or the "sending of God."

The ideas of Imago Dei and Missio Dei are closely linked together in Genesis 1.

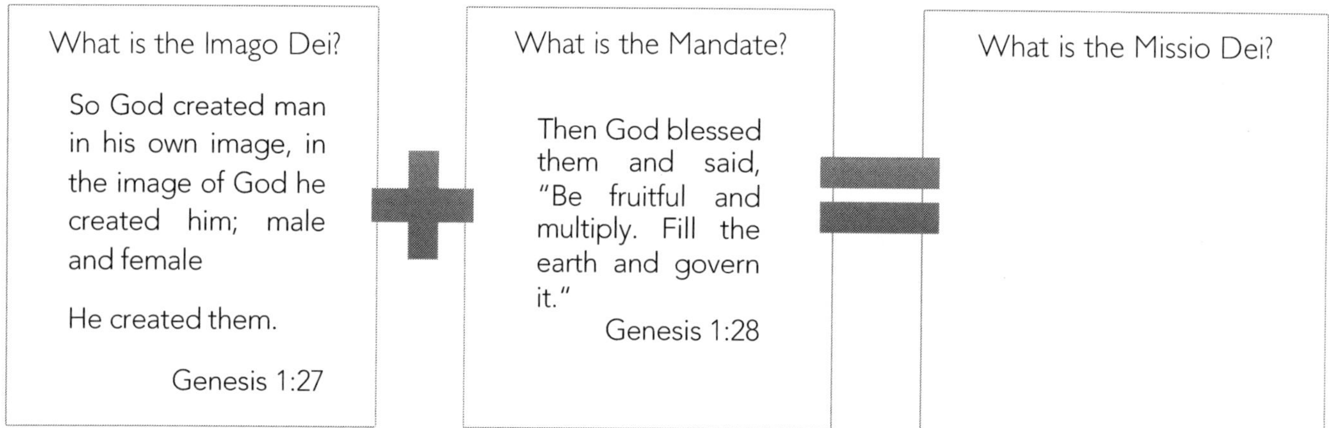

Then Jesus came to them and said, "All authority in heaven and on earth has been given to me. Therefore go and make disciples of all nations, baptizing them in the name of the Father and of the Son and of the Holy Spirit, and teaching them to obey everything I have commanded you. And surely I am with you always, to the very end of the age."

Matthew 28:19-20

What is the Missio Dei?

Tracing the Golden Thread through His Story.

How does the Bible describe God's glory?

God blessed them and said to them, "Be fruitful and increase in number; fill the earth and subdue it
Genesis 1:26

Why do you think that God chose to explain His glory in these ways?

and the priests could not perform their service because of the cloud, for the glory of the Lord filled the temple of God.

The Son is the radiance of God's glory and the exact representation of his being,

The city does not need the sun or the moon to shine on it, for the glory of God gives it light, and the Lamb is its lamp.

Praise his glorious name forever!
Let the whole earth be filled with his glory. Amen and amen!

The voice of the Lord is over the waters; the God of glory thunders, the Lord thunders over the mighty waters.

the glory of God, its radiance like a most rare jewel, like a jasper, clear as crystal

MISSION

How do I apply the Missio Dei to my life?

What are some things that distract or keep people from participating in the Mission of God?

What do I think?

What does my partner think?

How should this impact my life? *(head, hearts, hands, habits)*

What keeps me from participating in the mission of God?

Where are my circles of influence?

How will I respond?

Beliefs

Values

Actions

Habits

Mission

So whether you eat or drink or whatever you do, do it all for the glory of God.

1 Corinthians 10:31

How has God uniquely created me to reflect His glory?

So whether you eat or drink or whatever you do, do it all for the glory of God.
1 Corinthians 10:31

In the same way, let your light shine before others, that they may see your good deeds and glorify your Father in heaven.
Matthew 5:16

How do I like to help people?

What do I like learning about?

What do others see in me?

What am I interested in?

What experiences have impacted my life?

What am I good at?

Therefore, since we are surrounded by such a great cloud of witnesses, let us throw off everything that hinders and the sin that so easily entangles. And let us run with perseverance the race marked out for us, [2] fixing our eyes on Jesus, the pioneer and perfecter of faith. For the joy set before him he endured the cross, scorning its shame, and sat down at the right hand of the throne of God.

Hebrews 12:1-2

Mission

What happens when heaven and earth meet?

The color purple is created from two colors (red and blue) being mixed together. We are going to use it to symbolize two different elements that come together to form something that the Bible calls The Kingdom of God.

The Kingdom of God is the place where heaven and earth join together. The opening words of the Bible teach us that in the beginning, God created the heavens and the earth.

It was during this process that He created the material things that we see with our eyes and touch with our hands, and he created the immaterial or the supernatural things that we normally cannot see.

The Garden of Eden is the first place in the Bible where we see this joining of the material and the immaterial world. Genesis 3:8 tells us that God walked in the Garden with Adam and Eve.

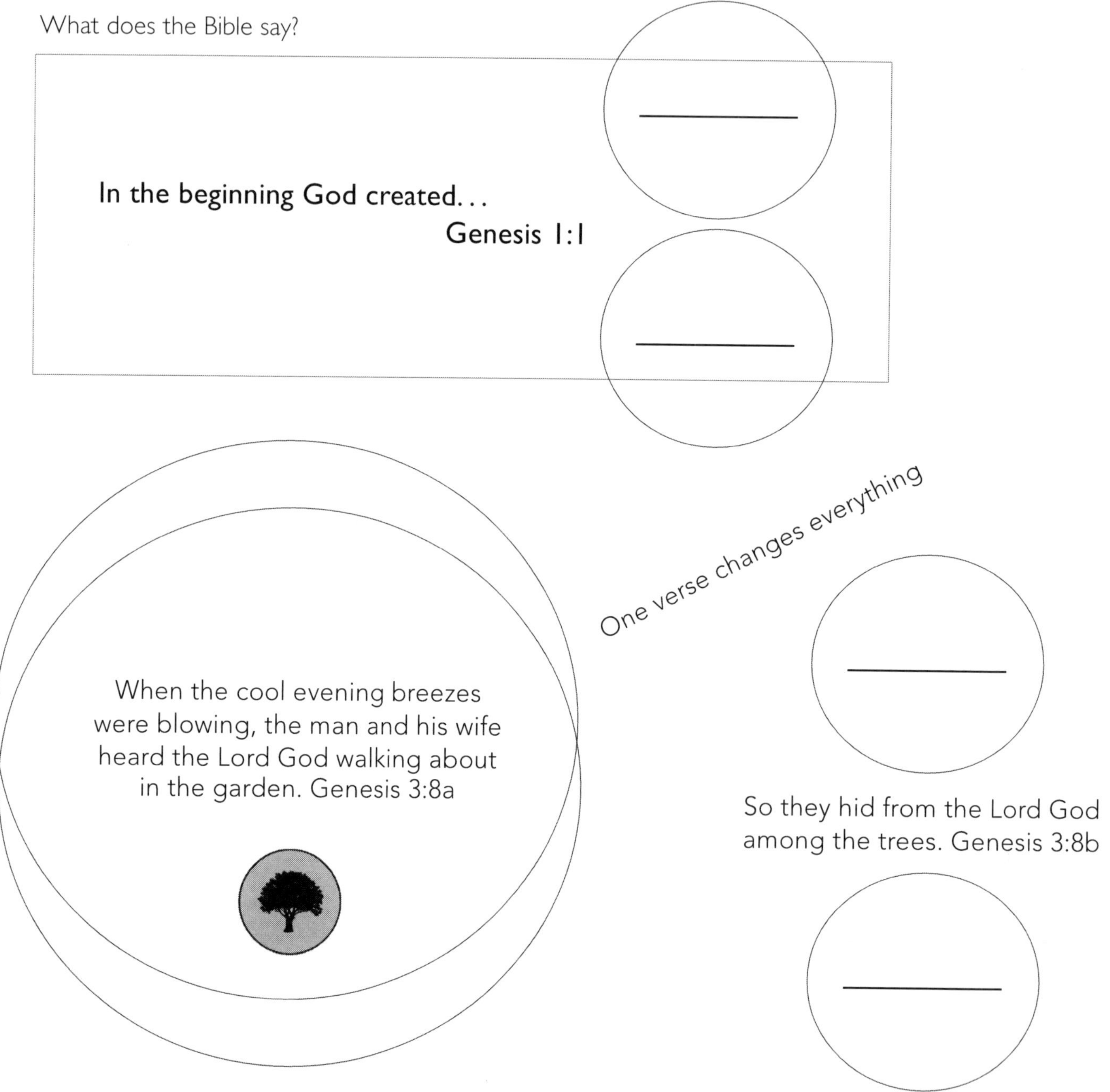

What happened in the garden? Genesis 1:26-3:24

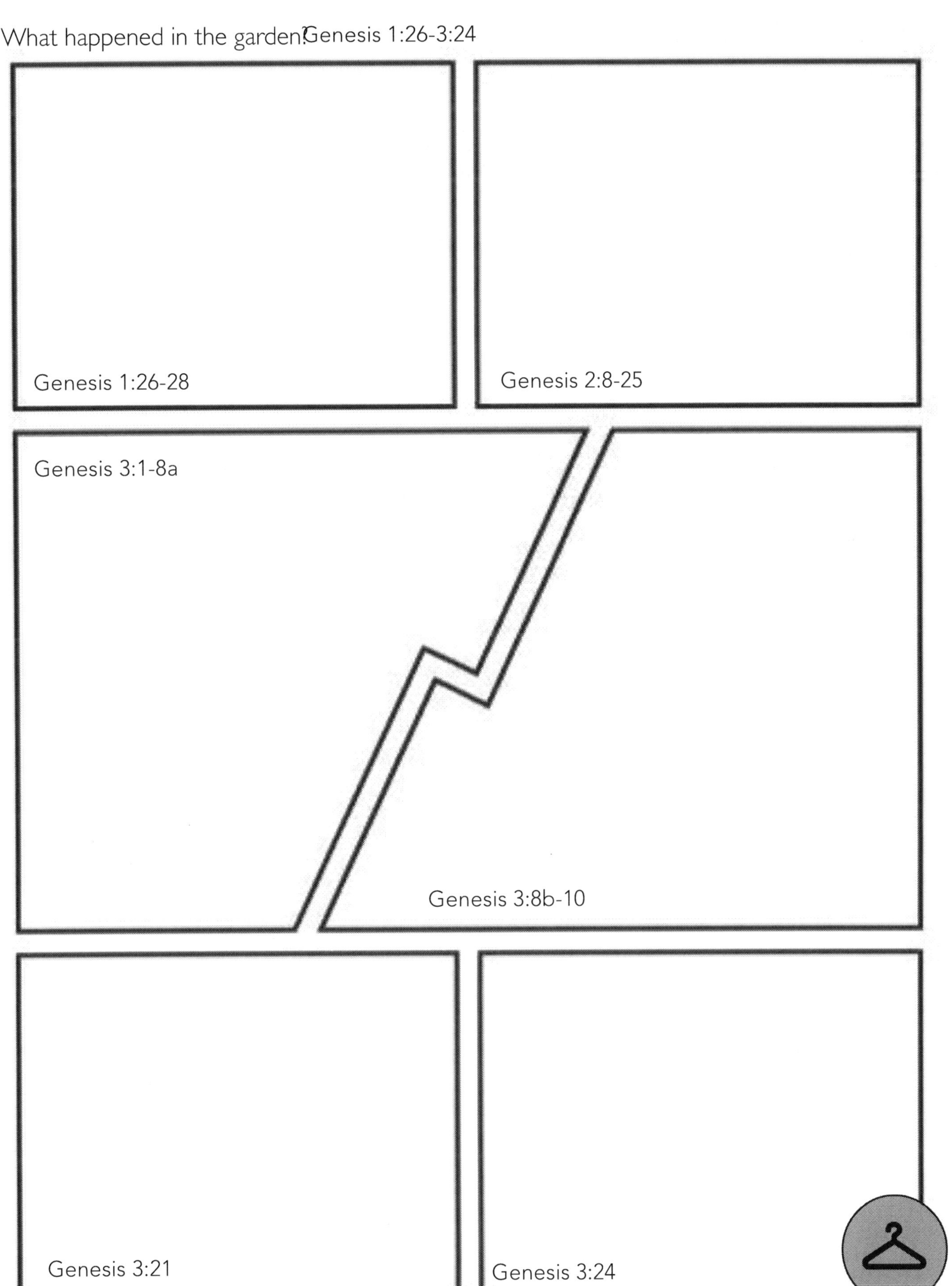

Compare and Contrast: What is the difference between sin and temptation?

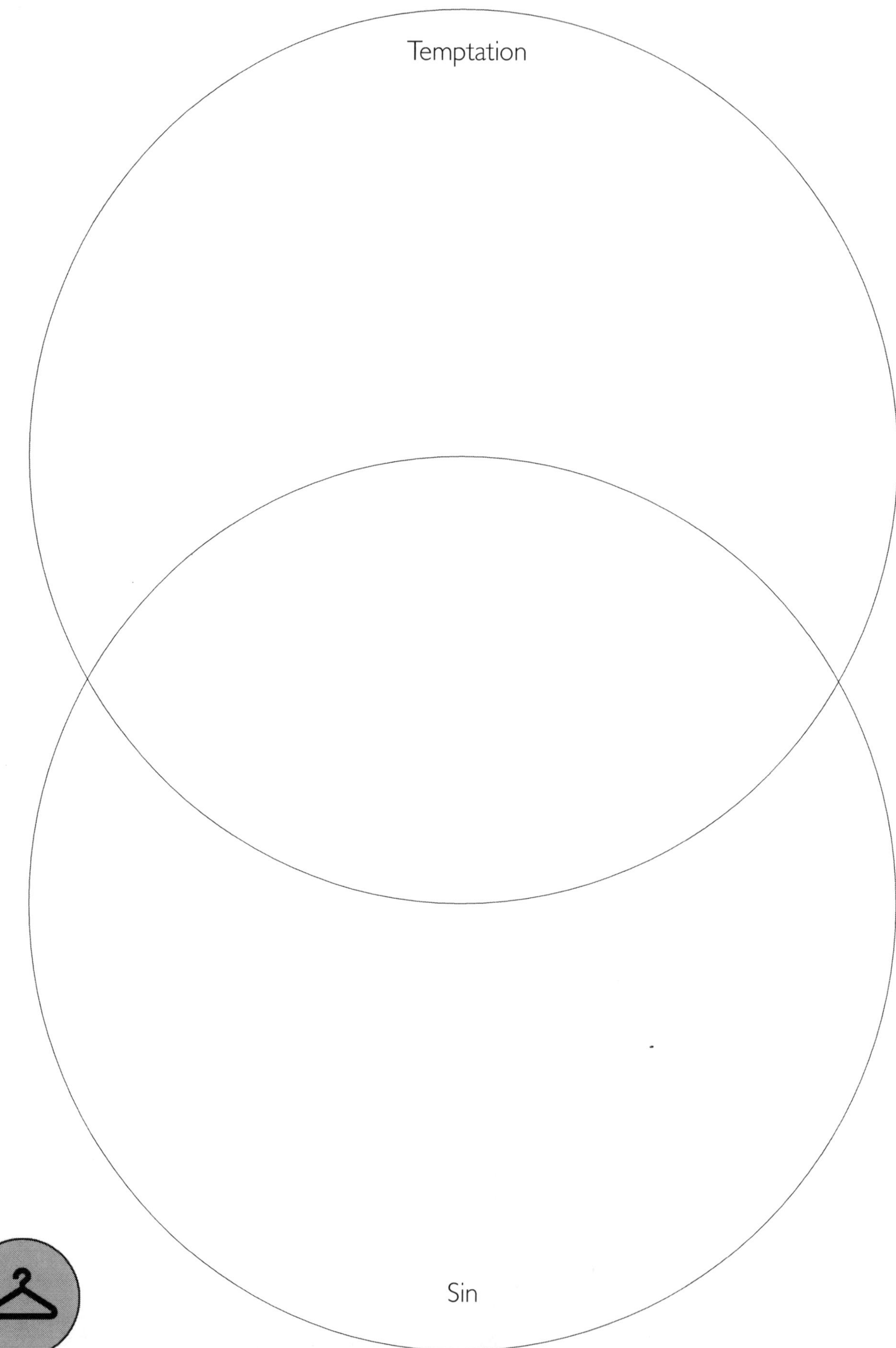

How do I understand the consequences of sin?
Compare. Contrast. Summarize

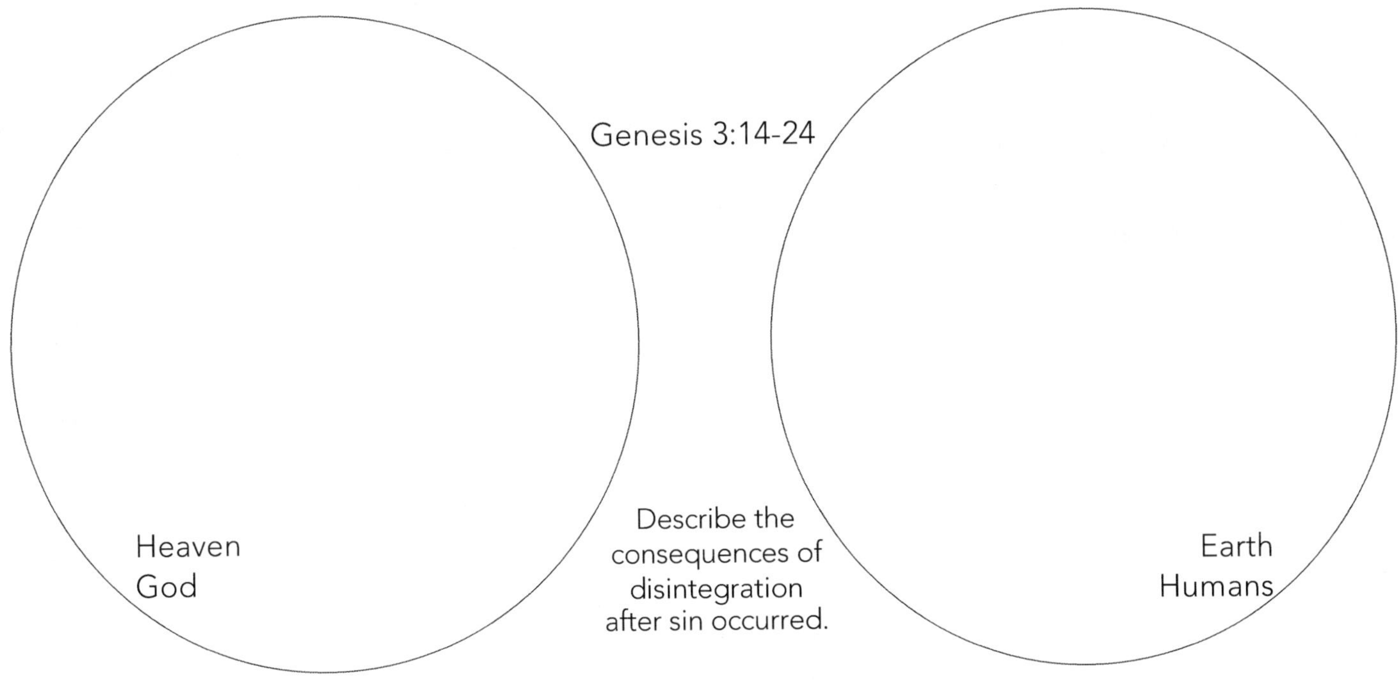

Now the man and his wife were both naked, but they felt no shame.
Genesis 2:25

Shame defined.

'a painful feeling of humiliation or distress caused by the consciousness of wrong or foolish behavior.'

At that moment their eyes were opened, and they suddenly felt shame at their nakedness. So they sewed fig leaves together to cover themselves.
Genesis 3:7

How do I make sense of shame?

What did Adam and Eve expect?

What actually happened?

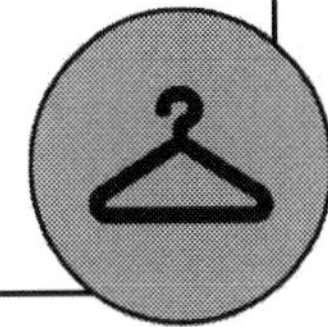

How do I understand Adam and Eve's motivation to rebel against God?

What did Adam fear?

What did Adam want?

What was the lie? What is the truth?

How do I understand my own motivation to rebel against God?

When faced with the temptation to follow God's will or follow my own what do I fear?

When faced with the temptation to reflect the glory of God or my own what do I want?

What is the lie?

How do I try to cover my shame?

Fear and shame lead to one of two responses

Self ____________________

[Adam] answered, "I heard you in the garden, and I was afraid because I was naked; so I hid." Genesis 3:10

Have you eaten from the tree that I [God] commanded you not to eat from?" Genesis 3:11

Self ____________________

The man said, "The woman you put here with me—she gave me some fruit from the tree, and I ate it." Genesis 3:12

The woman said, "The serpent deceived me, and I ate." Genesis 3:13

Shame & Separation. "I heard you walking in the garden, so I hid. I was afraid because I was naked." Genesis 3:10

Identifying and understanding the effects of the lie.

When I self promote what do I think will happen?

What actually happens?

When I self preserve what do I think will happen?

What actually happens?

Shame & Separation. "I heard you walking in the garden, so I hid. I was afraid because I was naked." Genesis 3:10

What is God's solution to the shame and separation caused by sin?

What was Adam and Eve's true problem?

Adam and Eve were trying to cover their ____________________ but what they really needed was to cover their ____________.

but you must not eat from the tree of the knowledge of good and evil, for when you eat from it you will certainly die."
Genesis 2:17

Think about it

What should Adam and Eve experienced after their rebellion?

What actually happens?

How do I understand God's grace?

Blood, Mercy, and Grace; what is the difference between religion and true worship?

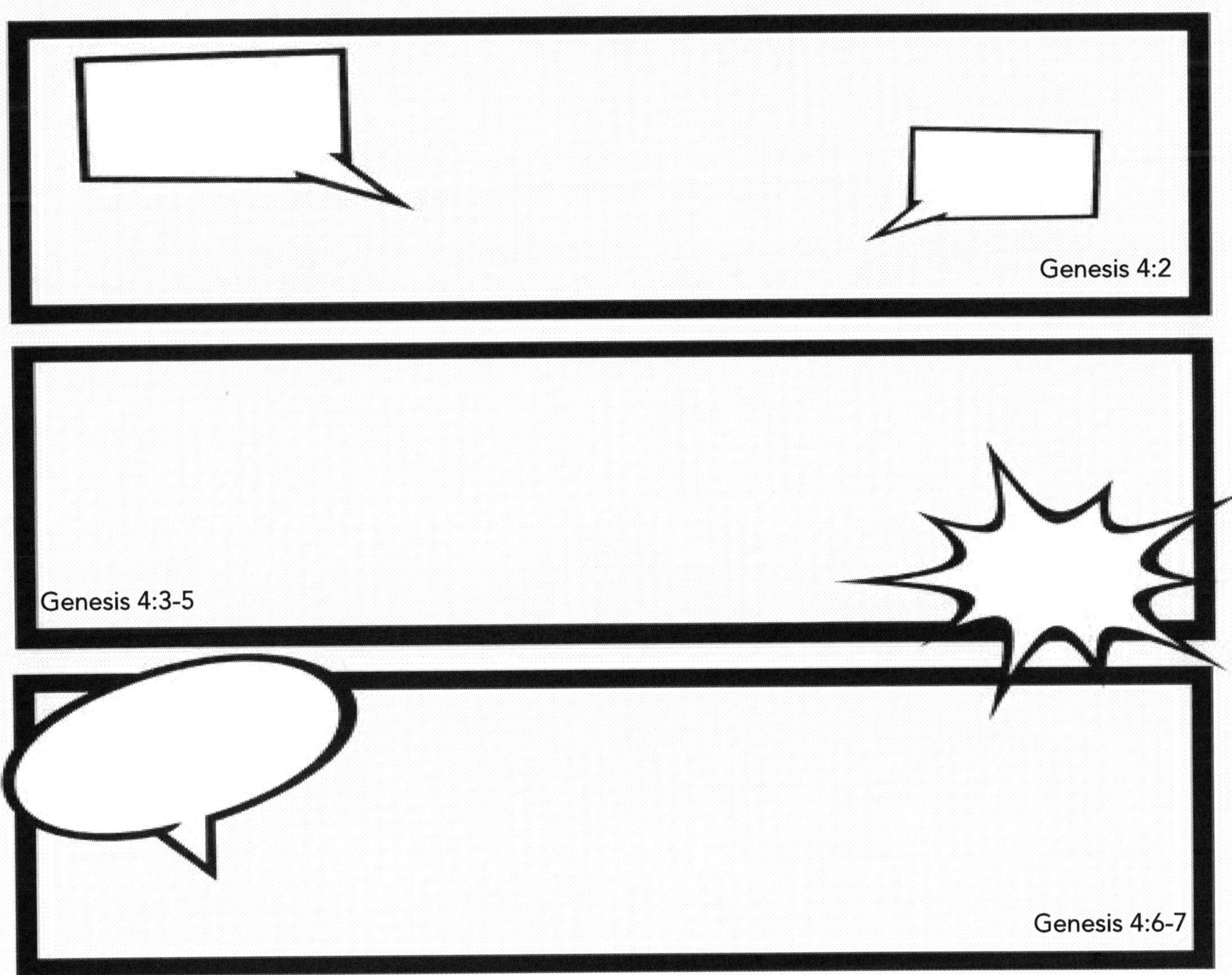

Genesis 4:8-16

It was by faith that Abel brought a more acceptable offering to God than Cain did. Abel's offering gave evidence that he was a righteous man, and God showed his approval of his gifts. Although Abel is long dead, he still speaks to us by his example of faith.
Hebrews 11:4

We must not be like Cain, who belonged to the evil one and killed his brother. And why did he kill him? Because Cain had been doing what was evil, and his brother had been doing what was righteous. 1 John 3:12

Is God evil?

Perhaps one of the most widely known and least understood events in the prologue is the story of Noah and The Ark. There are two primary misunderstandings on opposite sides of the spectrum.

The first misunderstanding is to equate the Ark to the pictures of the little boat with the cute animal heads sticking out of it. The second misunderstanding is to accuse God of being evil for wiping out nearly the entire population of the earth. After all, if we are to believe the majority of conventional narratives ...doesn't God wants to save everyone? So, what gives?

But let's be honest, no matter how cute, or adorable those little baby animals are, it is still kind of weird to decorate an infants room with pictures illustrating how God wiped out nearly all of humanity through a natural disaster.

If you were to place yourself on the spectrum of extremes, how you would assess your current understanding of Noah and the Ark?

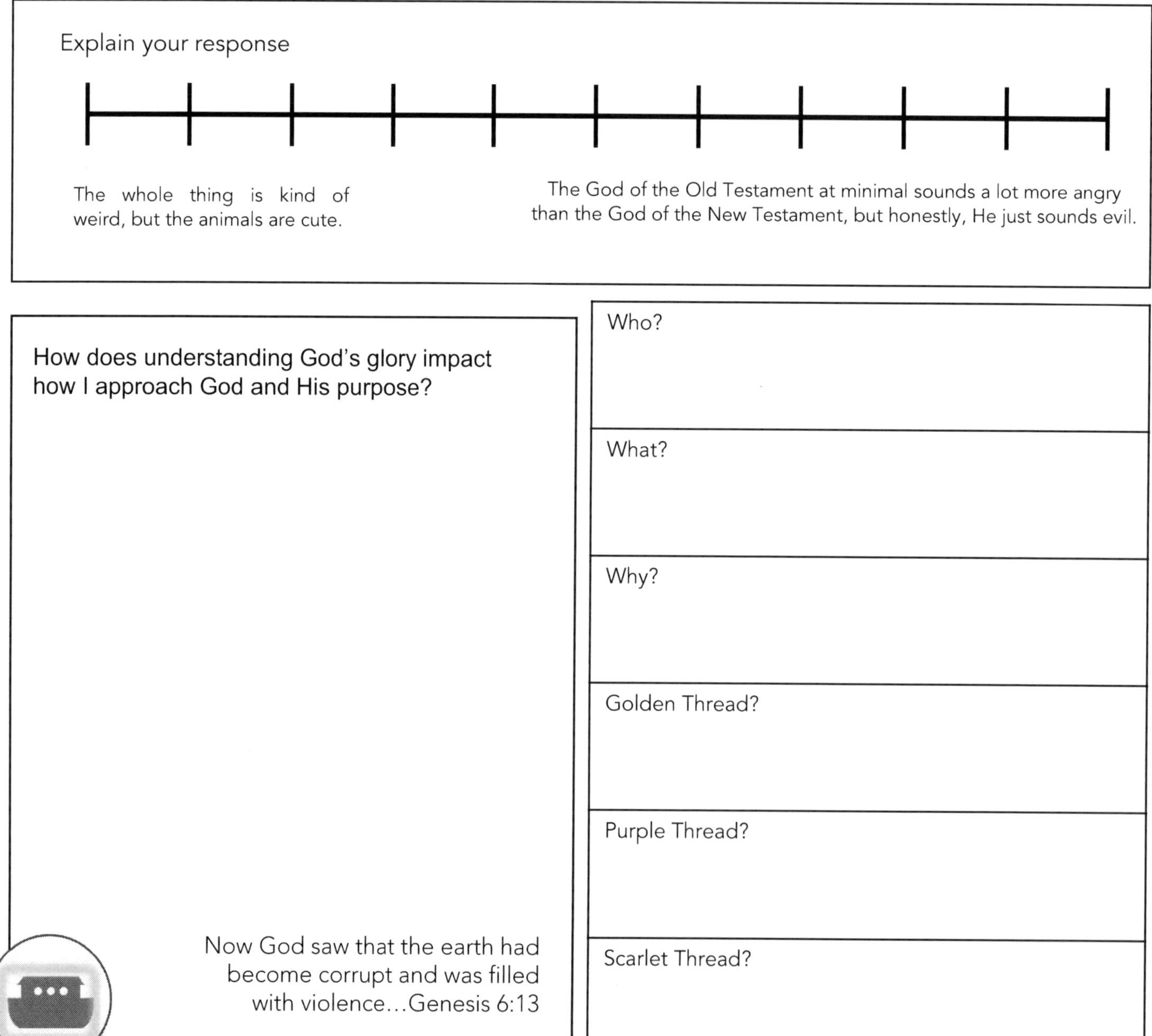

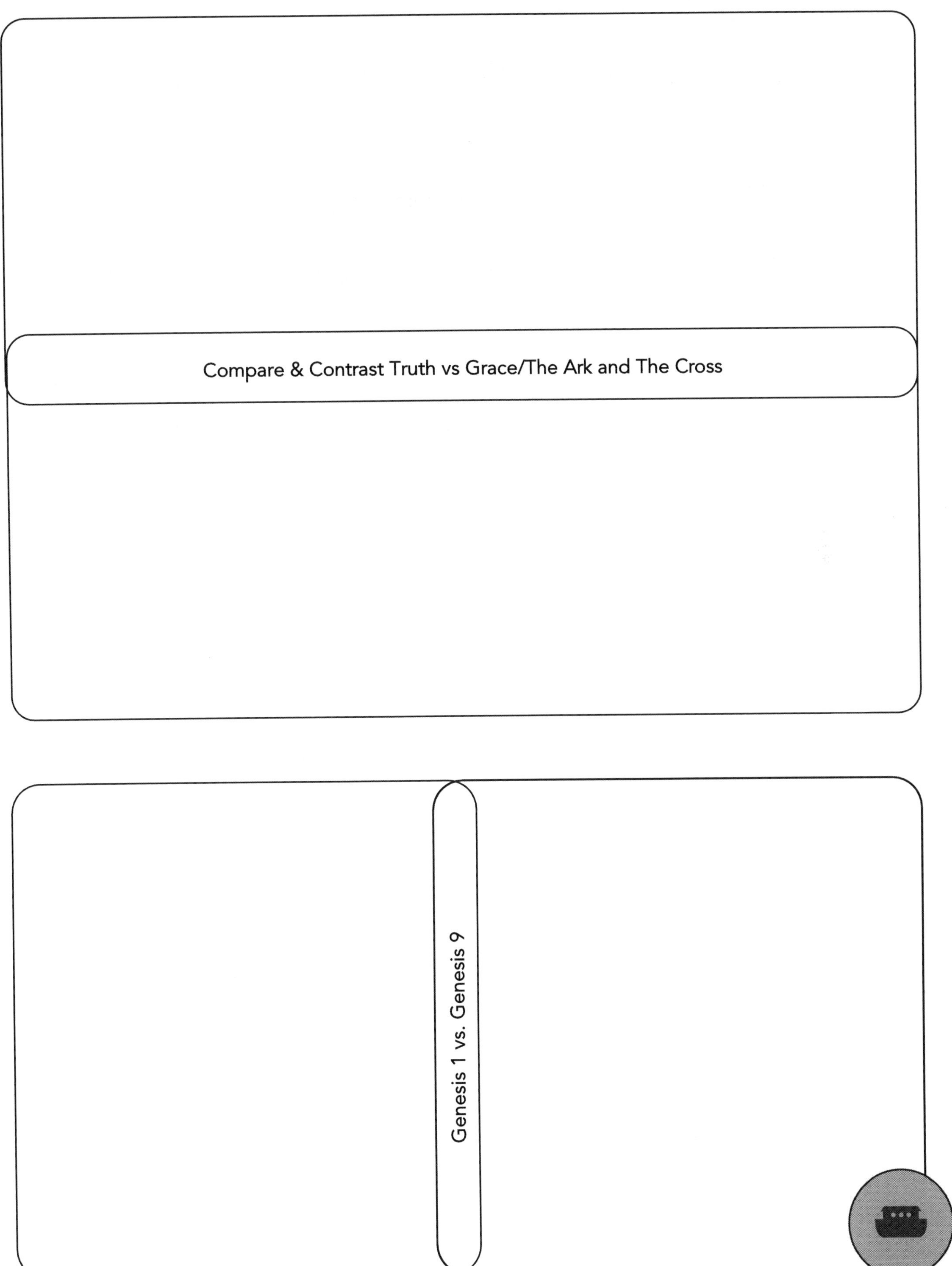
Compare & Contrast Truth vs Grace/The Ark and The Cross
Genesis 1 vs. Genesis 9

What happened at Babel?

Now the whole world had one language and a common speech. 2 As people moved eastward, they
found a plain in Shinar and settled there.

3 They said to each other, "Come, let's make bricks and bake them thoroughly." They used brick
instead of stone, and tar for mortar. 4 Then they said, "Come, let us build ourselves a city, with a
tower that reaches to the heavens, so that we may make a name for ourselves; otherwise we will be
scattered over the face of the whole earth."

5 But the Lord came down to see the city and the tower the people were building. 6 The Lord said, "If
as one people speaking the same language they have begun to do this, then nothing they plan to do
will be impossible for them. 7 Come, let us go down and confuse their language so they will not
understand each other."

8 So the Lord scattered them from there over all the earth, and they stopped building the city. 9 That is
why it was called Babel because there the Lord confused the language of the whole world. From
there the Lord scattered them over the face of the whole earth.

Genesis 11:1-9

What was the problem?

From one man he made all **the nations, that they should inhabit the whole earth**; and he marked out their appointed times in history and the boundaries of their lands. God did this **so that** they would **seek him** and perhaps reach out for him and find him, though he is not far from any one of us.
Acts 17:26-27

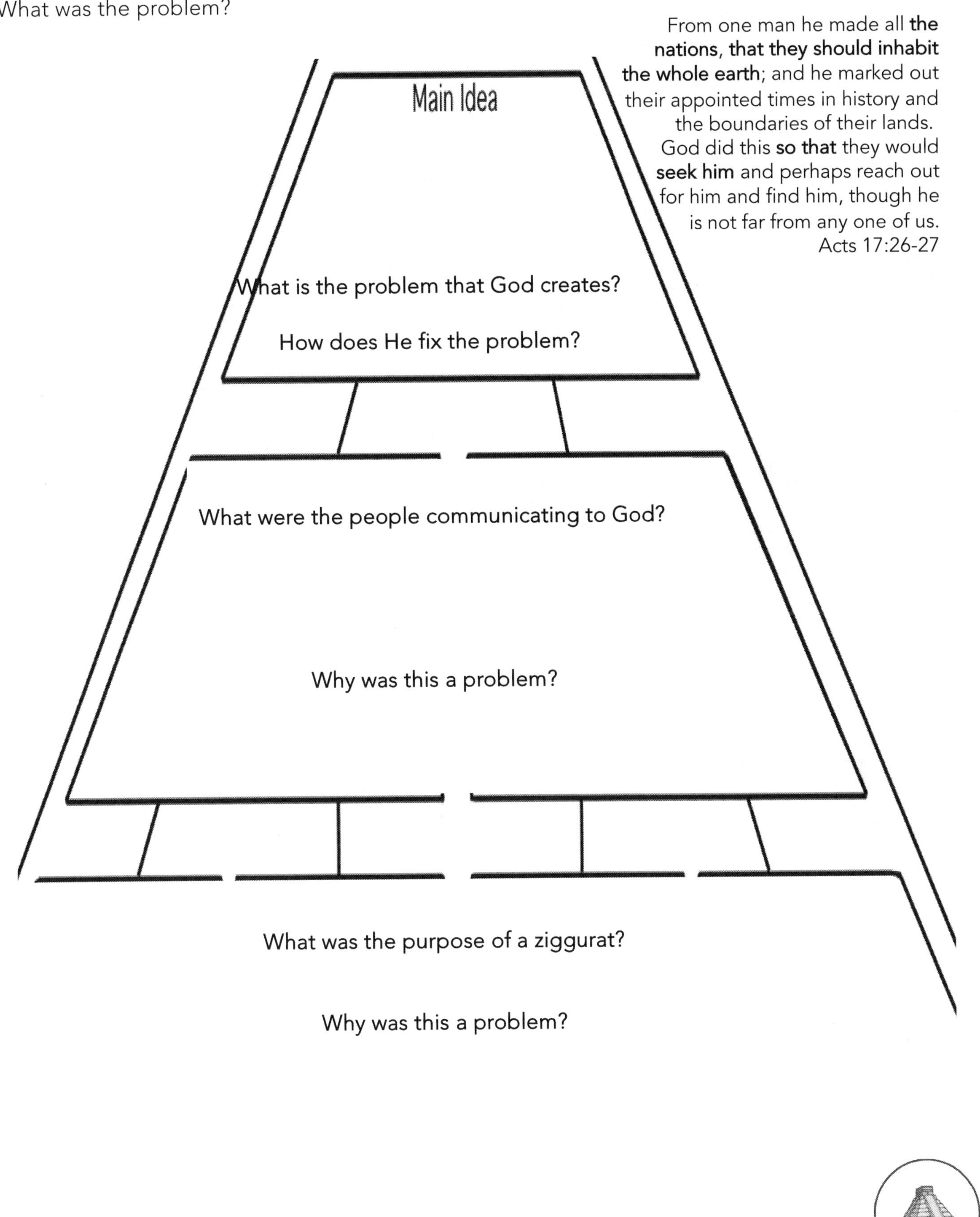

BABEL

COLLABORATION RUBRIC

Notes and Plans:

	Below Standard	Approaching Standard	At Standard	Above Standard
Takes Personal Responsibility for Learning and Contributing to the Learning Process	• Is not prepared, informed or ready to contribute to the team • Does not utilize technology as agreed upon • Does not participate in project tasks • Does not listen to or use feedback to improve work	• Usually prepared, informed and ready to work with team • Does not utilize technology according to agreed upon standards with consistency • Needs reminding or prompting to complete tasks • Uses some feedback and complete most tasks	• Prepared and ready to work • Well informed and cites evidence that encourages learning among other team members • Consistently uses technology as agree upon • Self motivated and does not need to be reminded to complete tasks • Completes tasks on time • Evaluates and uses feedback to improve work	
Contribution to the Team	• Does not help the team to solve problems; may be the source of problems for the team • Does not ask probing questions, express ideas, or elaborate in response to questions or discussions • Do not offer help • Does not provide useful feedback	• Cooperates but does not actively participate in problem solving • Occasionally asks probing questions, expresses ideas, or elaborates in responses or discussions • Sometimes offers help • Sometimes provides feedback but it may not always be helpful	• Helps the team to solve problems and manage conflict • Clearly expresses ideas, asks probing questions, listens to others and solicits feedback from quiet team members to ensure that all perspectives are shared and heard • Provides useful feedback • Identifies opportunities to help others where appropriate	
Relationships and Respect	• Impolite or unkind to team members (may interrupt, ignore, talk over or use hurtful words or body language) • Does not listen or respect other perspectives	• Usually polite and kind to team members • Usually listens and respects team members • Disagrees with content, perspectives and opinions without attacking the person	• Polite and kind to team members • Listens to, acknowledges and respects other team members • Disagrees with content and builds community by affirming the person	

HISTORY

THE MISSION OF GOD

AND THE SECRET OF THE GOLDEN THREAD

patriarchs

Can God be trusted?

Learning to love God's Word

The Lord had said to Abram, "Go from your country, your people and your father's household to the land I will show you. "I will make you into a great nation, and I will bless you; I will make your name great, and you will be a blessing. I will bless those who bless you, and whoever curses you I will curse; and all peoples on earth will be blessed through you."

Genesis 12:1-3

What is the learning goal for Patriarchs?

Patriarch can generally refer to any older, respected male, specifically one who is the head of a family. In the Bible, it is narrowly defined to include, Abraham, Isaac, and Jacob as the heads of the people of Israel.

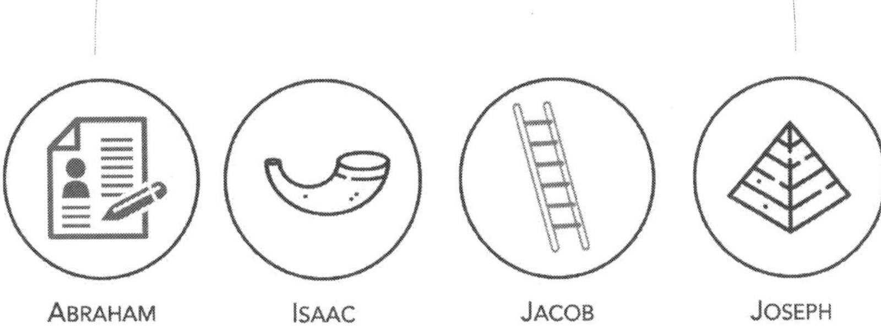

- Afraid,
- Ambition,
- Anxious,
- Demanding,
- Dishonest,
- Doubtful,
- Faithless,
- Foolish,
- Impatient,
- Inconsiderate,
- Jealous,
- Lazy,
- Restless,
- Irrational,
- Deceptive,
- Selfish

Imagine receiving a text or an email from someone that you did not know, but they were "applying" for the opportunity to be your friend.

They explained that they had many desirable characteristics for friendship, including the ones listed to the left of this paragraph.

After reading through their list...
how would you respond to their offer of friendship? Why?

Would you be excited?

Would you be scared?

In Isaiah 41:8, God refers to Abraham as His friend.

Abraham is a friend of God, and yet after you study his life and examine his character, you may wonder how that is possible.

The list on the left side of this page are all words that describe the men in the Bible known as the Patriarchs of Israel (Abraham, Isaac, and Jacob).

In this unit, we will examine the question, who are the Patriarchs of the Biblical plot, how do they relate to God and others and what can we learn from their faith, fears, and failures?

Patriarchs; The story continues

Setting:
Where:

When:

Major Characters:

Minor Characters:

Plot/Problem:

Event 1:

Event 2:

Event 3:

Outcome:

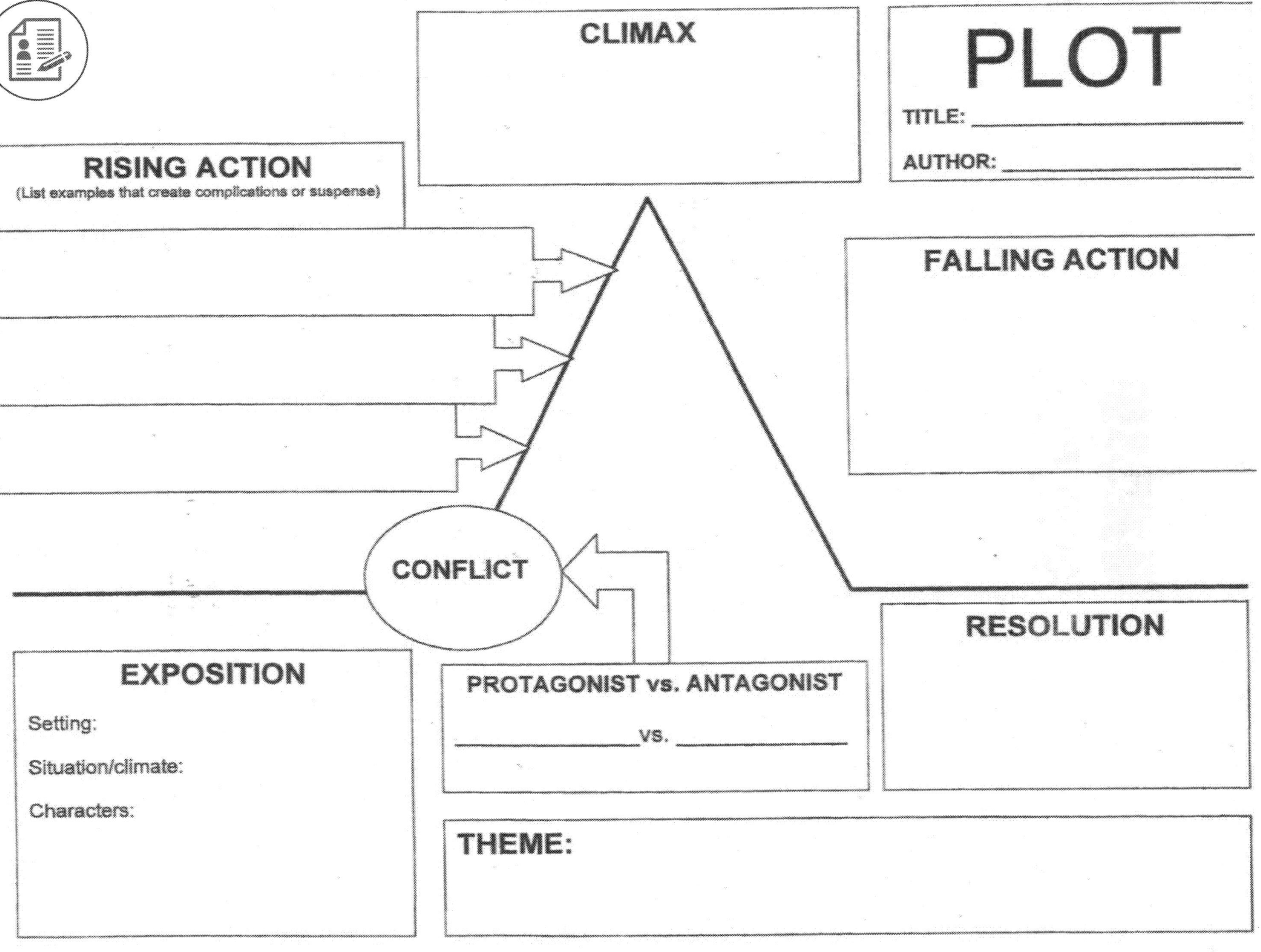
PLOT
TITLE:
AUTHOR:
CLIMAX
RISING ACTION
(List examples that create complications or suspense)
FALLING ACTION
CONFLICT
RESOLUTION
EXPOSITION
Setting:
Situation/climate:
Characters:
PROTAGONIST vs. ANTAGONIST
vs.
THEME:

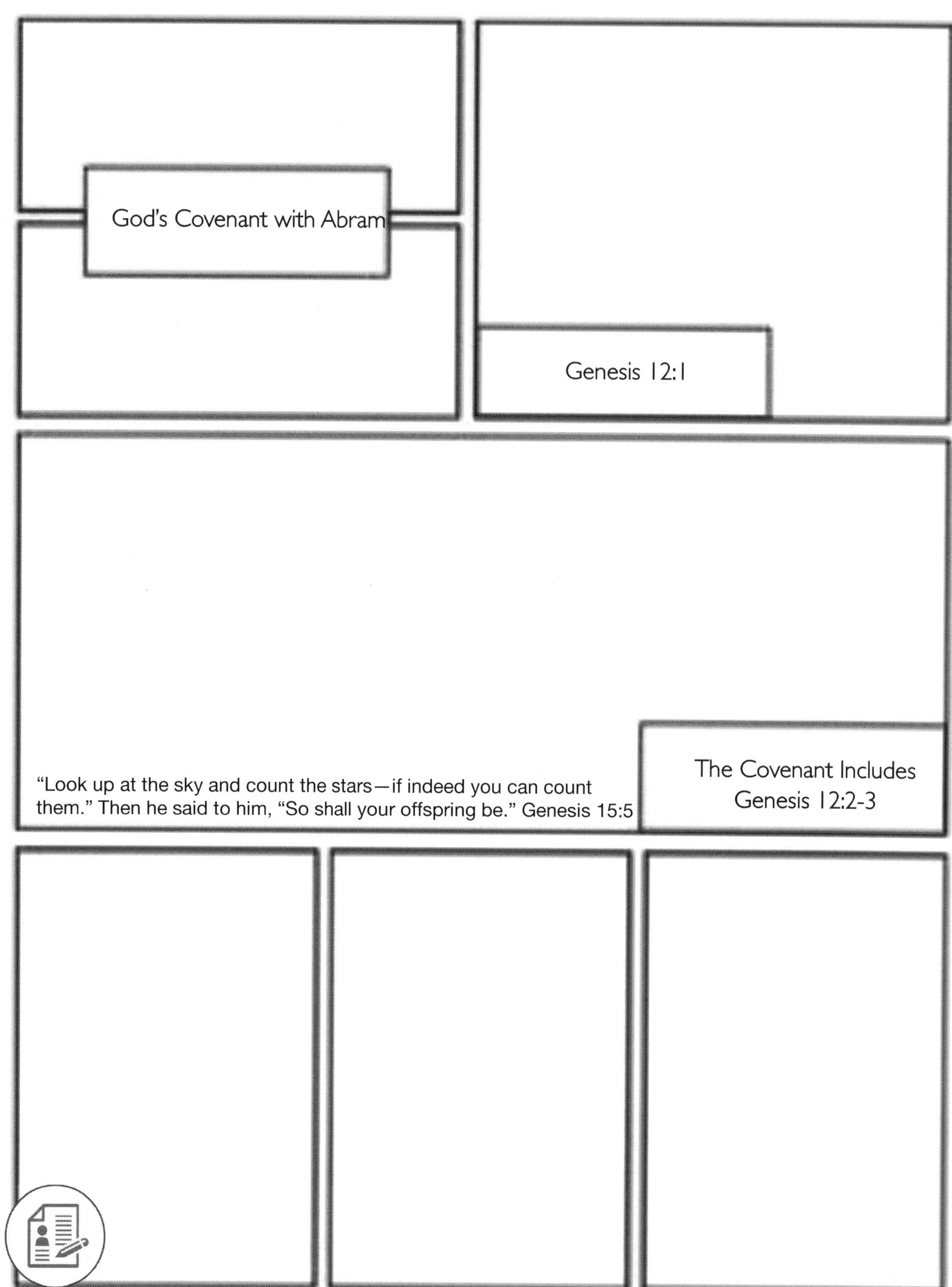
God's Covenant with Abram
Genesis 12:1
"Look up at the sky and count the stars—if indeed you can count them." Then he said to him, "So shall your offspring be." Genesis 15:5
The Covenant Includes
Genesis 12:2-3

How do Abraham & Sarah Respond?

Genesis 12:4-20

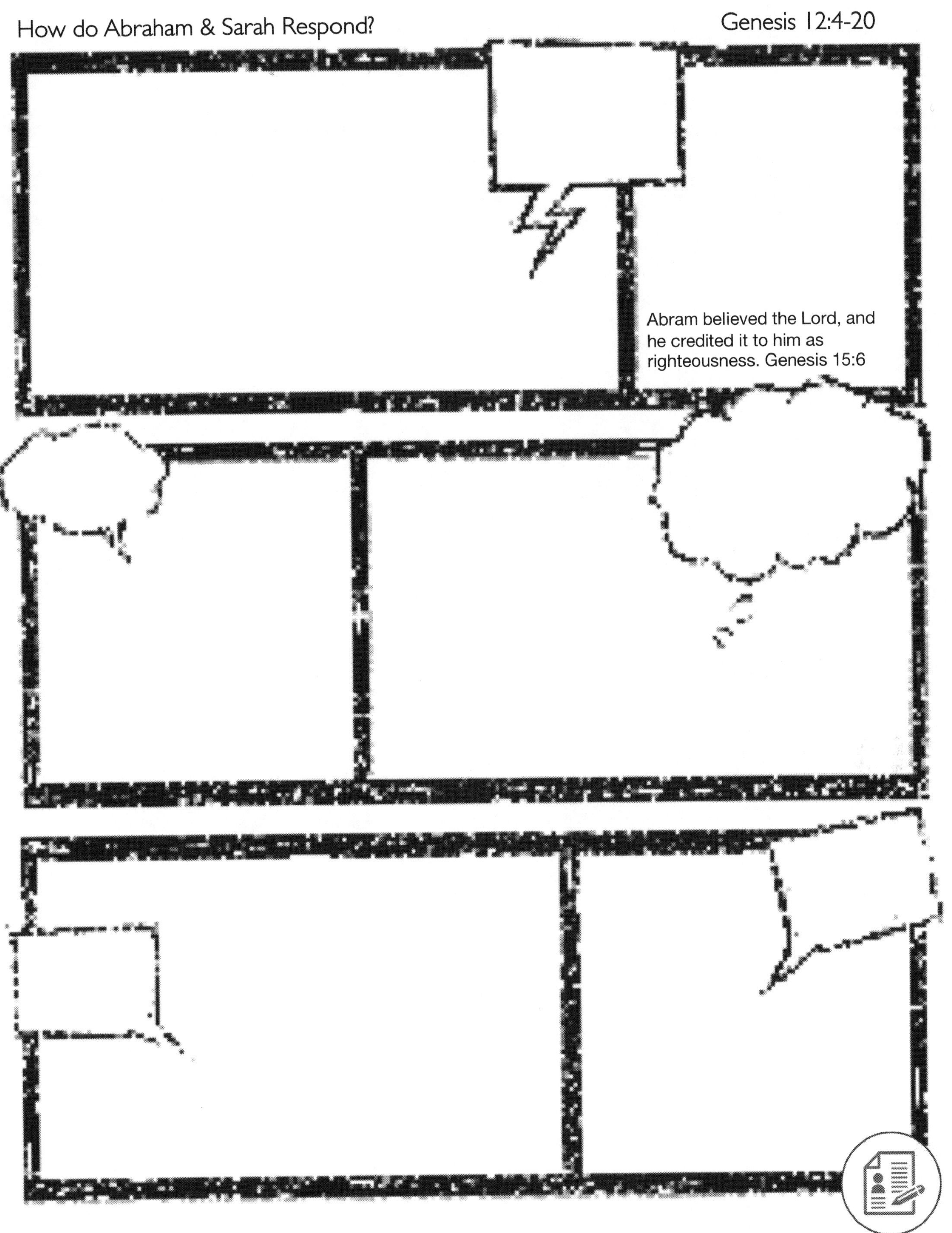

Explain and Illustrate

1. Gihon Spring
2. Tigris River
3. Euphrates River
4. Mediterranean Sea
5. Dead Sea
6. Nile River
7. Red Sea

1. Ur
2. Canaan
3. Egypt
4. Wilderness

1. Mount Moriah
2. Mount Sinai
3. Mount Nebo

"I am the Lord, who brought you out of Ur of the Chaldeans to give you this land to take possession of it." Genesis 15:7

10 Now there was a famine in the land, and Abram went down to Egypt to live there for a while
because the famine was severe. 11 As he was about to enter Egypt, he said to his wife Sarai,
"I know what a beautiful woman you are. 12 When the Egyptians see you, they will say, 'This is
his wife.' Then they will kill me but will let you live. 13 Say you are my sister, so that I will be
treated well for your sake and my life will be spared because of you." Genesis 12:10-13

What can I learn? What is the paradox in Abraham's failure to trust God?

What can I apply?

In what ways is my relationship with God similar? Different? Why?

BELIEFS

VALUES

ACTIONS

HABITS

Explain and Illustrate: Genesis 16:1-16

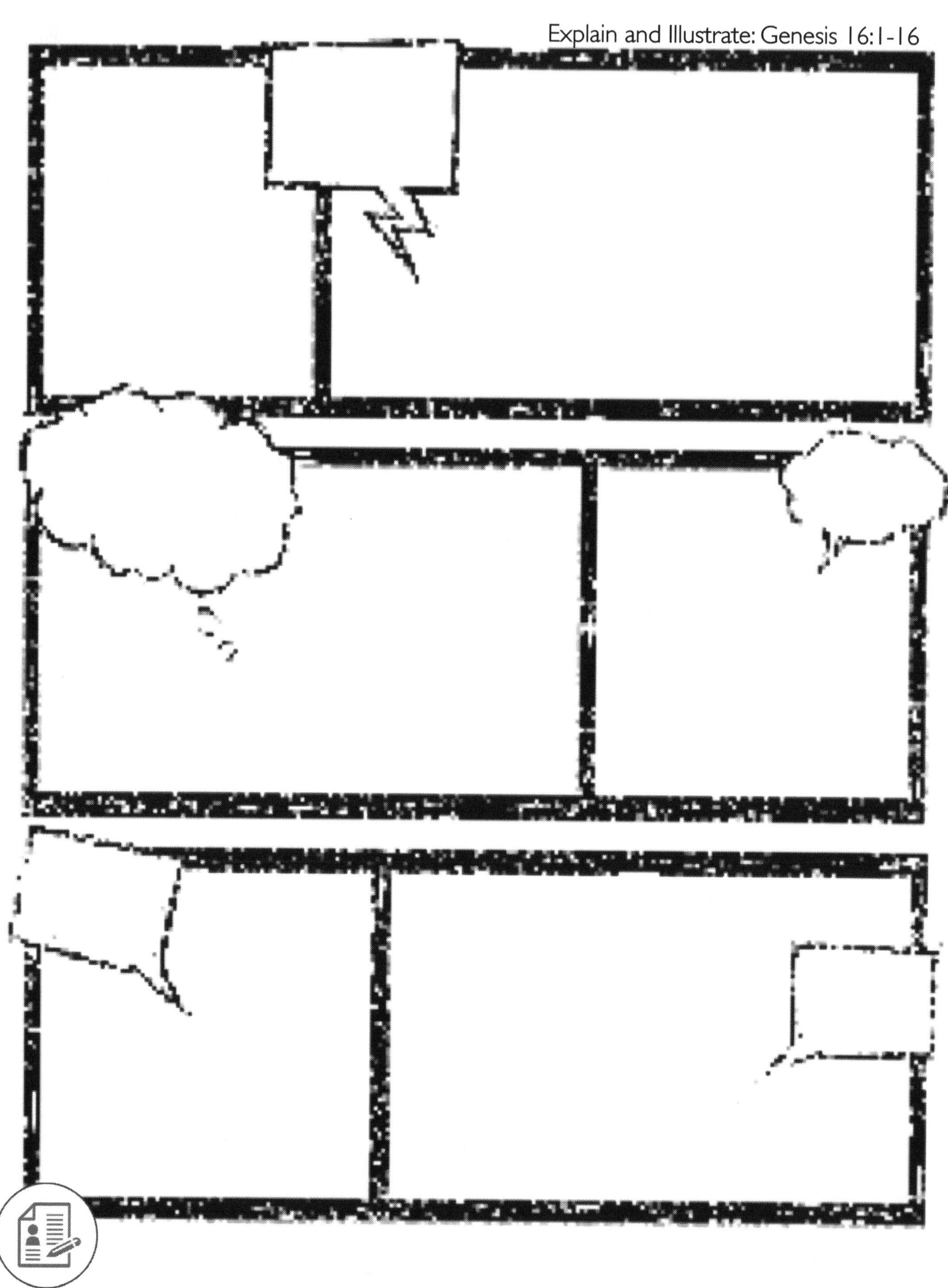

Explain and Illustrate: Genesis 17:15-22, 18:1-15

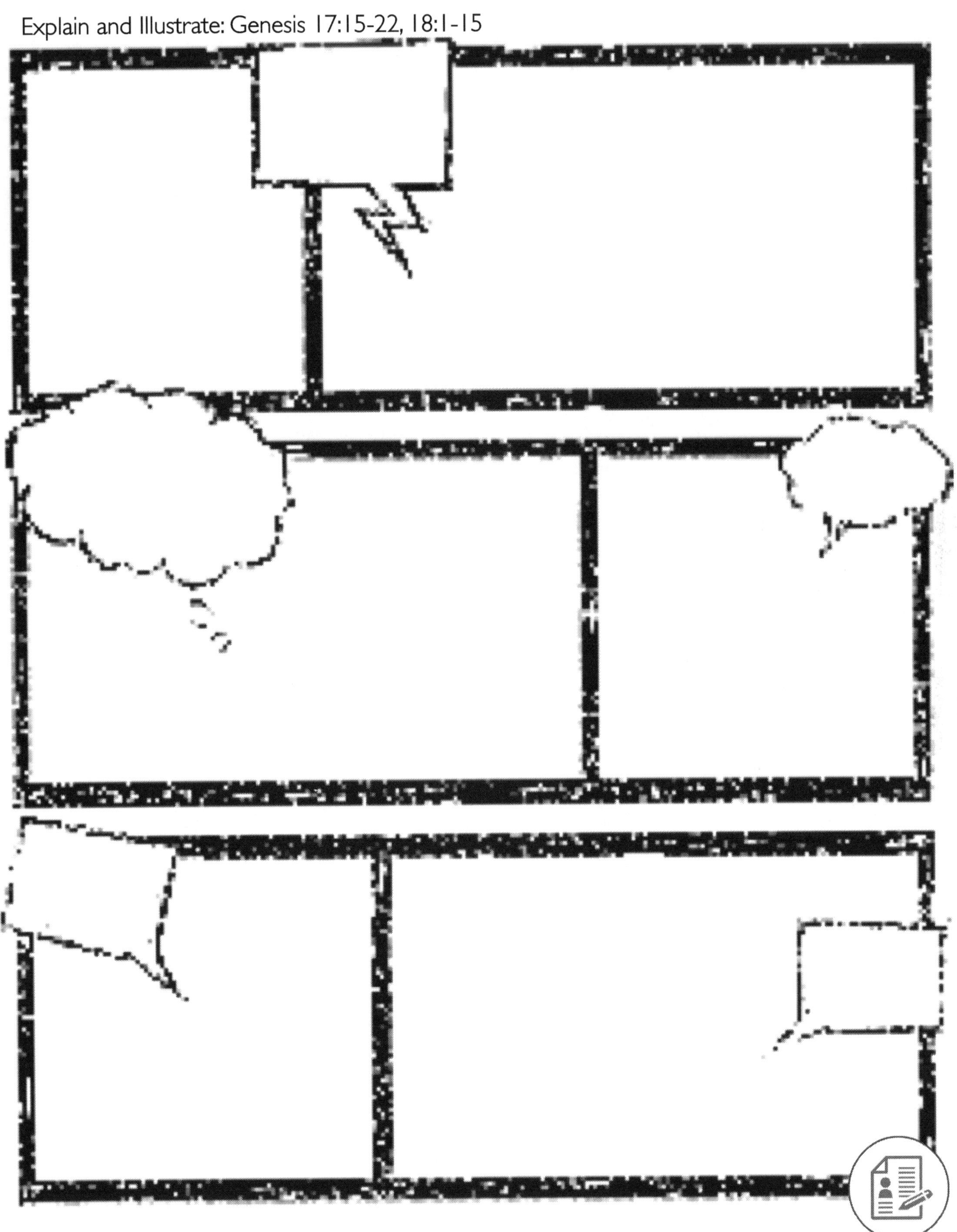

Explain and Illustrate Genesis 20:1-15

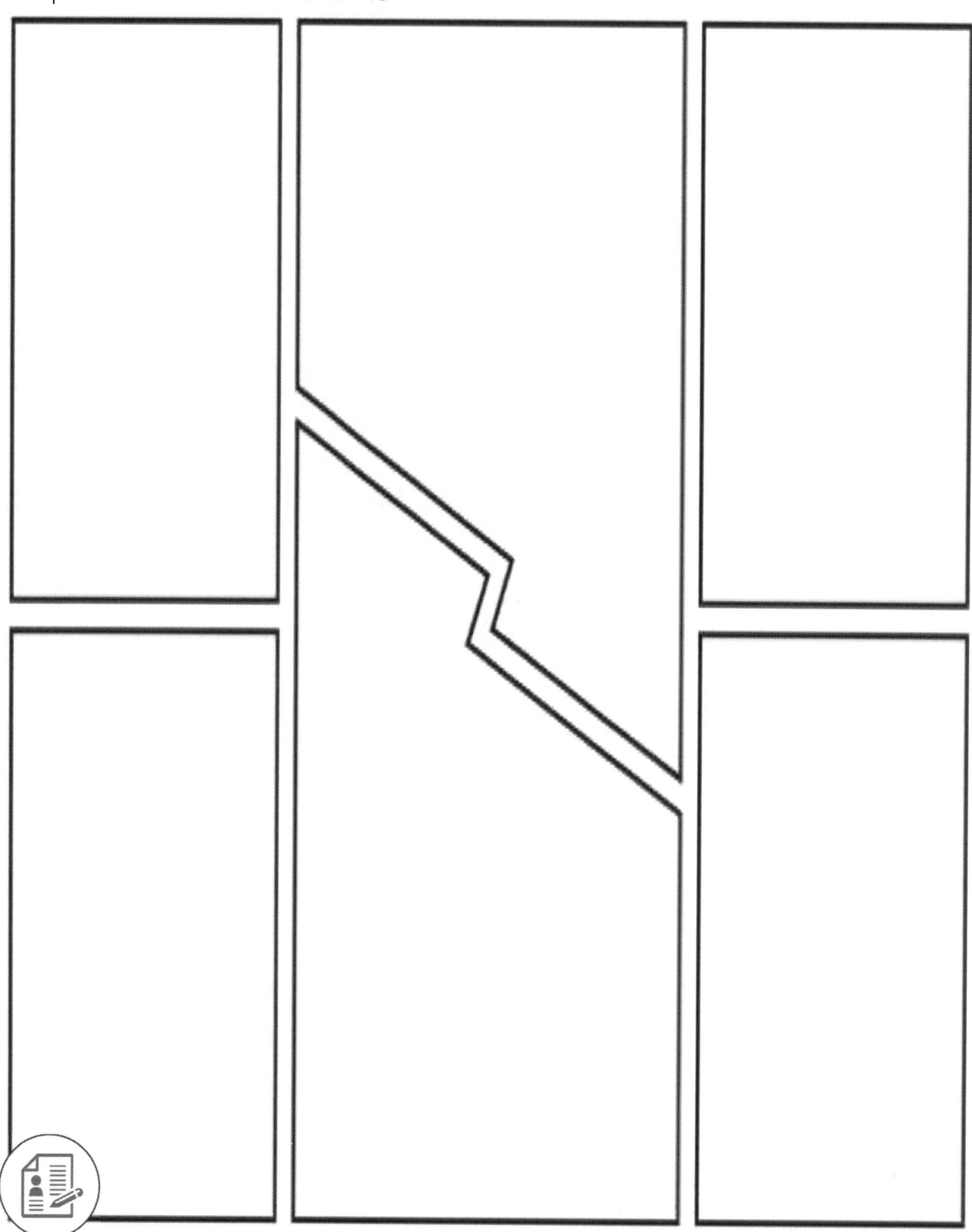

Abraham, Isaac, Ishmael

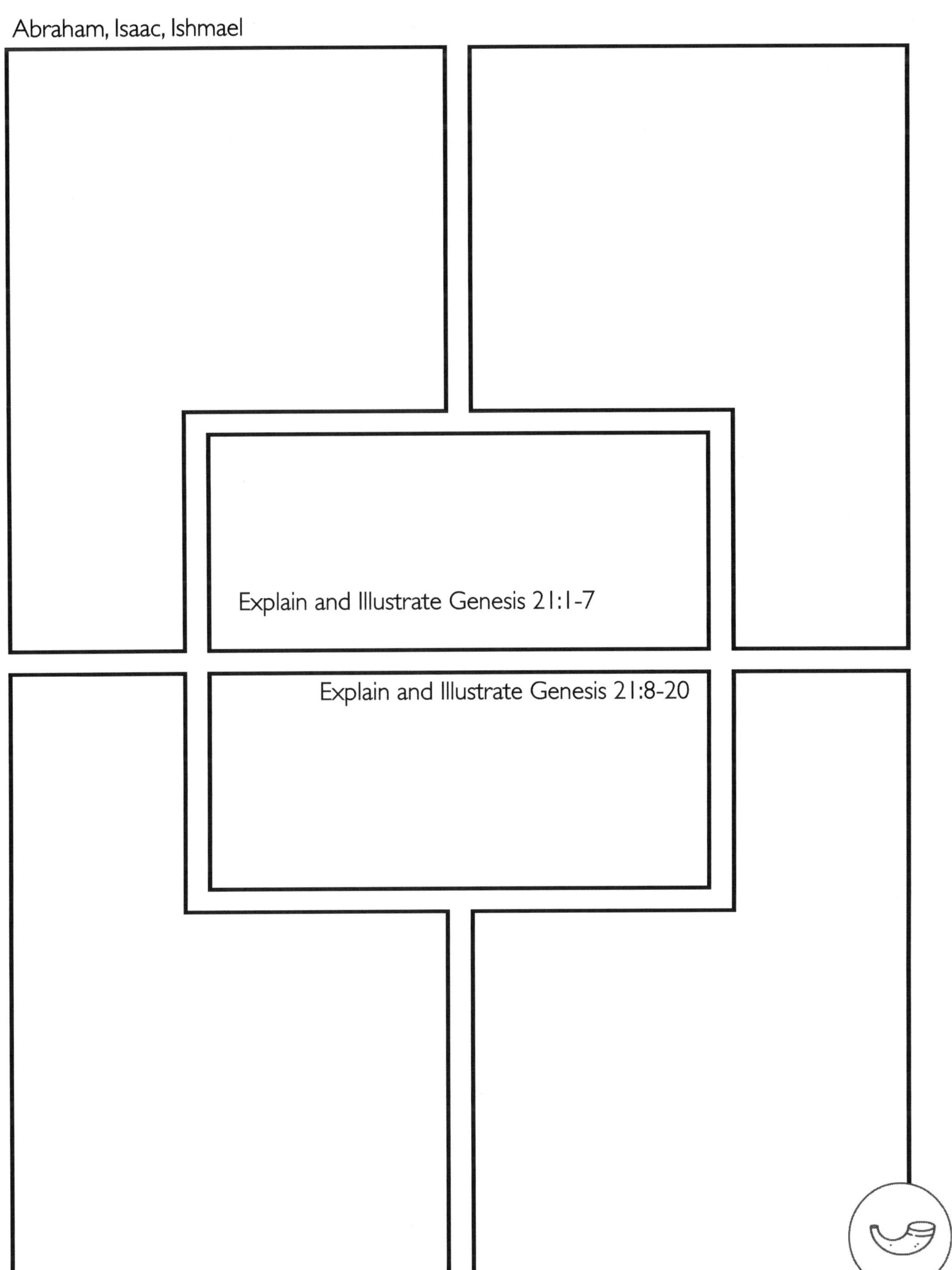

Explain and Illustrate Genesis 22:1-19

Jehovah Jireh: The Lord who provides
Genesis 22:12-4

The meaning of this name is The Lord Who Provides. The name is literally, The Lord Who Sees, or *The Lord Who Will See To It.*

The one who will see to our needs and provide for us. Jehovah-Jireh means; the Lord Who will see to it that my every need is met because He sees.

He is able to meet my fully need in just the right time.

For Abraham, it was the ram caught in the thicket that was offered in Isaac's place.

Character Study. Abram; Man of faith?

Examine the paradox of Abram's continued failure to trust God and his acts of obedience and faith?

Words

Thoughts

Actions

Character

What does this reveal to us about Abram?

What does this reveal to us about God?

What does this reveal to us about myself?

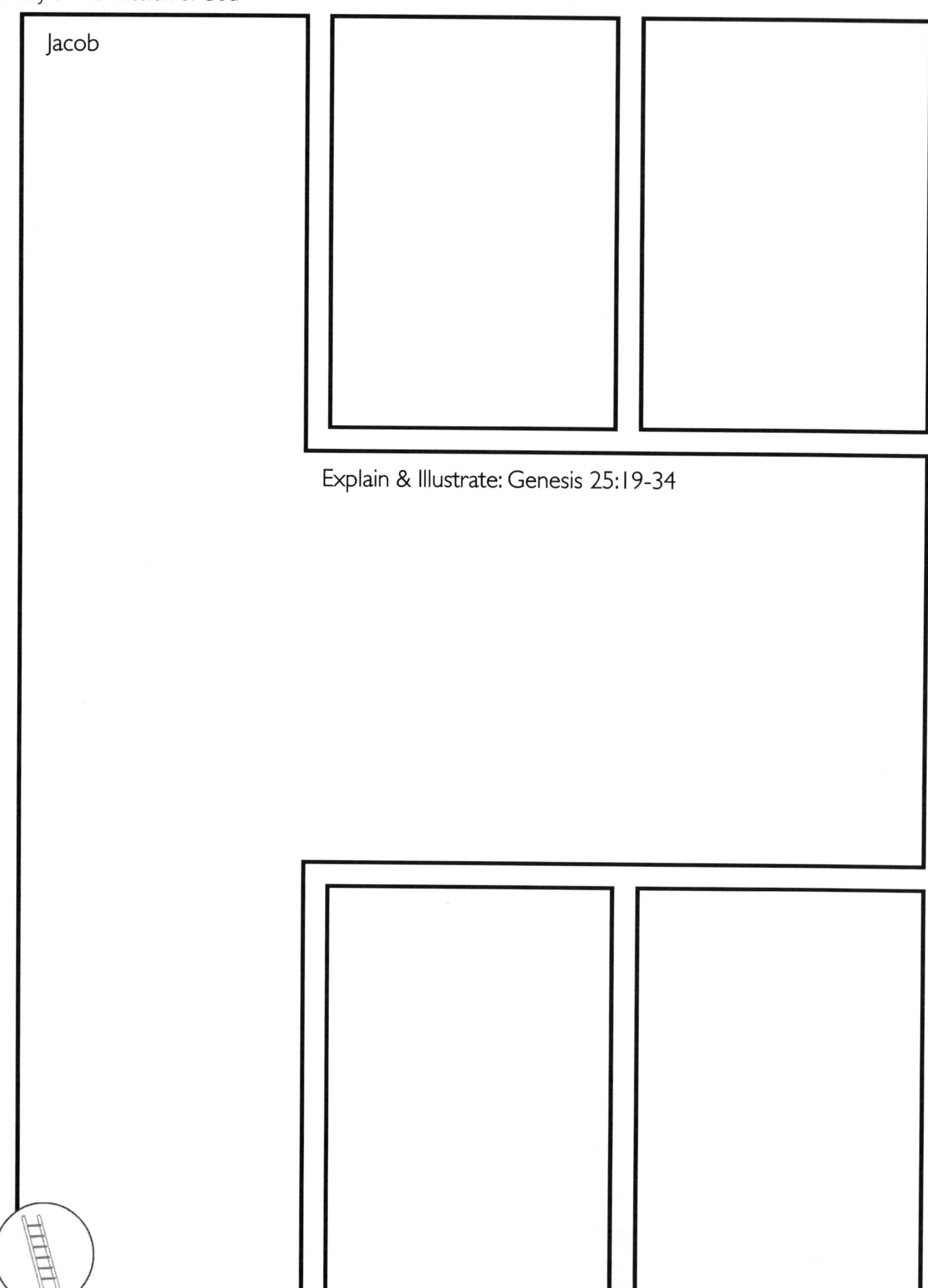
Jacob
Explain & Illustrate: Genesis 25:19-34

Israel
Explain & Illustrate: Genesis 28:10-22
Explain & Illustrate: Genesis 32

Joseph: Genesis 37
Joseph: Genesis 39
Joseph: Genesis 40

You intended to harm me, but God intended it for good to accomplish what is now being done, the saving of many lives.
Genesis 50:20

Joseph: Genesis 45

"What you intended for evil…

Joseph: Genesis 42

Joseph: Genesis 41

Character Study. Jacob; Man of faith?

Examine the paradox of Jacob continued deception and fear with his acts of obedience and faith?

Words

Thoughts

Actions

Character

What does this reveal to us about Jacob?

What does this reveal to us about God?

What does this reveal to us about myself?

Character Study. Joseph; Man of faith and forgiveness

Examine the paradox of Joseph continued fall into the pit his acts of obedience and faith?

Words

Thoughts

Actions

Character

What does the life of Joseph teach me about forgiveness?

BELIEFS

VALUES

What does this reveal to us about God?

ACTIONS

What does this reveal to us about myself?

HABITS

Can God be trusted?

What do the lives of the Patriarchs and their families teach us bout trusting God?

Make two lists. In the first list, you should include all of the ways that the lives of the Patriarchs and Matriarchs and their families demonstrated trust and faith in God amid obstacles, trials, and temptations. In the second list include times that you observe them demonstrating fear rather than faith.

Think. Pair. Share.

Identify and list the results of their choices to fear rather than practice faith.

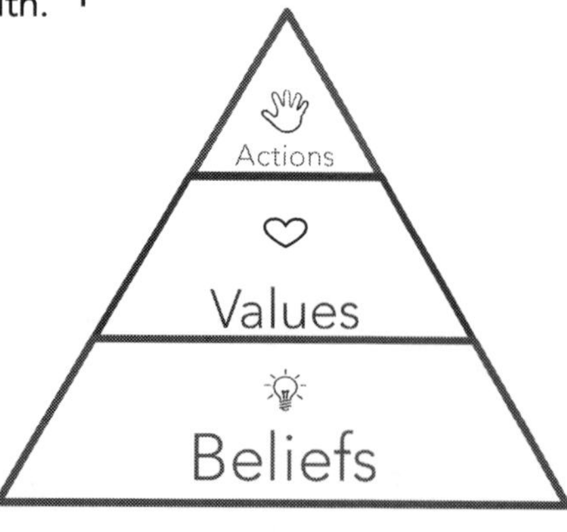

Trust

Fear, Faith and Focus

What can I learn by observing how these individuals related to God?

What can I apply?

In what ways is my relationship with God similar? Different? Why?

If beliefs influence values and values influence actions then what do I believe, value and do based on my perspective of whether or not I can trust God with my life?

BELIEFS

VALUES

ACTIONS

HABITS

Patriarch Character Study Project

Choose one of the patriarchs or matriarchs of the nation of Israel and conduct a character study of their lives, relationships, choices, and the consequences.

Part I. Research. Use specific references to identify:

- Thoughts
- Actions
- Character traits and attributes
- Enemies (perceived or real)
- Choices
- Obstacles
- Trials, Temptations, Fears
- Victories
- Failures (personal)
- Failures (defeat)

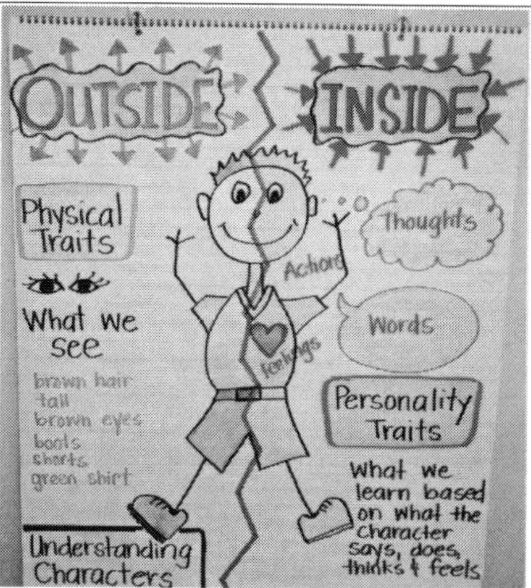

Who are the major and minor characters that influence their lives?

What are common or reoccurring choices, fears, patterns, or events in the life of this character?

How does the Bible describe them physically? (Tall, short, hairy, smooth, handsome, charming).

What is the setting around the life of the character, and how did the setting influence their lives?

What are three key plot points in the life of your character, and how did your character respond to them?

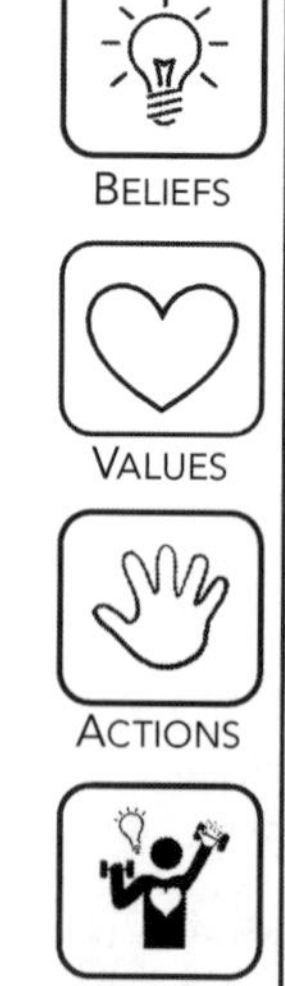

What does your character believe? (about themselves, about God)

What do the actions of your character reveal about what they value?

What habits (good or bad) influence the decisions and actions of this character

Part II. Do an initial drawing of your character that applies the research that you have conducted.

Emotions

- Describe how does a character feel (and a certain moment in the plot.
- Identify multiple feelings and multiple different points in the plot
- What emotion is the character experiencing.
- Anger, nervous, surprised. upset, embarrassed, excited?

Traits

- Describe the personality of the character.
- How does the character usually behave?
- Are they… kind, bossy, determined, outgoing, friendly, shy, mean, daring, reckless, compassionate?

Character Trait Bank

Ablen	Demanding	Hopeless	Restless
Active	Dependable	Humorous	Rich
Adventurous	Depressed	Ignorant	Rough
Affectionate	Determined	Imaginative	Rowdy
Afraid	Discouraged	Impatient	Rude
Alert	Dishonest	Impolite	Sad
Ambitious	Disrespectful	Inconsiderate	Safe
Angry	Doubtful	Independent	Satisfied
Annoyed	Dull	Industrious	Scared
Anxious	Dutiful	Innocent	Secretive
Apologetic	Eager	Intelligent	Selfish
Arrogant	Easygoing	Jealous	Serious
Attentive	Efficient	Kindly	Sharp
Average	Embarrassed	Lazy	Short
Bad	Encouraging	Leader	Shy
Blue	Energetic	Lively	Silly
Bold	Evil	Lonely	Skillful
Bored	Excited	Loving	Sly
Bossy	Expert	Loyal	Smart
Brainy	Fair	Lucky	Sneaky
Brave	Faithful	Mature	Sorry
Bright	Fearless	Mean	Spoiled
Brilliant	Fierce	Messy	Stingy
Busy	Foolish	Miserable	Strange

Calm	Fortunate	Mysterious	Strict
Careful	Foul	Naughty	Stubborn
Careless	Fresh	Nervous	Sweet
Cautious	Friendly	Nice	Talented
Charming	Frustrated	Noisy	Tall
Cheerful	Funny	Obedient	Thankful
Childish	Gentle	Obnoxious	Thoughtful
Clever	Giving	Old	Thoughtless
Clumsy	Glamorous	Peaceful	Tired
Coarse	Gloomy	Picky	Tolerant
Concerned	Good	Pleasant	Touchy
Confused	Grateful	Poor	Trusted
Considerate	Greedy	Popular	Unfriendly
Cooperative	Grouchy	Positive	Unhappy
Courageous	Grumpy	Precise	Upset
Cross	Happy	Proud	Warm
Cruel	Harsh	Quick	Weak
Curious	Hateful	Quiet	Wicked
Dangerous	Healthy	Rational	Wise
Daring	Helpful	Reliable	Worried
Dark	Honest	Religious	Wrong
Deceptive	Hopeful	Responsible	Young

Patriarchs Character Study and "Sculpture"

How to create a Patriarch Sculpture

1. Blow up a balloon so that it is a approximately the size, or a little smaller than you want your head to be.

2. Add your base. Fill a tin can 1/3 full of sand. Use masking tape to connect the balloon inside the can on all sides. Be sure to smooth down the masking tape if there are bumps. This will serve as a neck to your head.

3. Make the paste. Mix 1 part water with 1 part flour.

    - Most recipes suggest 2 parts water to 1 part flour, but you want this to be a little thicker for the head but feel free to dilute with if it helps to make it easier to work with.

4. Tear newspapers into 2 by 6 inch (5 by 15 cm) strips. Tear a few larger squares and set them aside. Note: Work outside or on a drop cloth as you begin forming the head.
5. Dip a newspaper strip into the thick flour and water mix. Smooth the paper strips onto your balloon. Work with 1 strip at a time until you cover the entire head and the can.
6. Allow the can and the balloon to dry completely (24-48 hours to be safe).
7. Cover with a second layer of newspaper strips dipped in the flour and water mixture.
8. Allow to dry and repeat 2 more times. You should have completed 4 costs of strips on the head and give them the opportunity to dry completely.
9. Use the larger pieces of newspaper to form nose, ears or other features that you would like to highlight. Connect them using the masking tape as you pinch the paper into the desired shape.
10. Smooth the masking tape very well using a wooden spoon to ensure that the tape is smooth in every area. Dip larger squares of newspaper into the Mache mixture and smooth 1 layer over the features. Allow them to dry.
11. Cover the head (options)
    - Spray with a light coat of spray adhesive and cover with fabric
    - Paint the head with colored paint. (Use spray paint for quicker application)
    - For detailing the face use different colors of paints to create and highlight different features.
12. Allow time to dry and then accessorize.

Final Deliverables

1. Character Study and Analysis Poster (Wall Worthy)

2. Character Sculpture

3. 2-3 paragraph character description describing the character and telling the major plot points from their lives.

    Note that #3 will be displayed next to the Sculpture at the Museum

Supply List

Smock or oversized paint shirt
Tin can (empty and clean)
Balloon
Shredded newspaper
Flour
Water
Masking Tape
Paints or spray paint
Drop cloth
Foam paint brush(es)

HISTORY

THE MISSION OF GOD

AND THE SECRET OF THE GOLDEN THREAD

passover

Can God be trusted?

Learning to love God's Word

We have heard how the Lord dried up the water of the Red Sea for you when you came out of Egypt . . . When we heard of it, our hearts melted in fear and everyone's courage failed because of you, for the Lord your God is God in heaven above and on the earth below.

Joshua 2:10a, 11

What is the learning goal for Passover?

Passover is one of the most sacred holidays for the people of Israel. It would later take on new and additional meaning for the followers of Christ.

PASSOVER

JOSEPH MOSES PLAGUES PASSOVER

In Genesis 15, God informs Abraham that there will be a time in the future when his descendants would be enslaved in Egypt for 400 years.

When Joseph and his brothers (the 12 tribes of Israel) we brought to Egypt, things were in position for that prophecy to be fulfilled.

Threatened by their presence and their numerical growth, the Egyptians would enslave the people of Israel and subject them to increased levels of cruelty.

In the minds of the people of Israel, the question became, had God forgotten? Would the God of Abraham remember His descendants and keep His promise?

What happens next is a story of epic proportions. It is the type of story that Hollywood studios could only dream of and when retold accurately, it has blockbuster potential.

A fact that has proven true time and time again as Hollywood has attempted to tell and retell the story of the Exodus.

The Passover portion of the plot of God's History is the story of how God raises a man to deliver the children of Israel from slavery.

And in the process God sends a message to the world that there is no god like the God of Abraham, Isaac, and Jacob.

The Passover Project

Many museums have interactive videos that help illustrate specific time periods or concepts. Your assignment is to make an interactive video that will help your audience better understand the timeline and purpose of the Passover in the life of the people of Israel from the perspective of our four major threads.

To accomplish this project you need to make a retro screen feel trendy again. Your creativity in this project is needed and encouraged.

Part I. You will research the story via film to study and understand the major elements of the plot, characters and the motifs.

Part II. You will research the story from the historical narrative of Scripture to separate fact from the elements that were "made for the movie."

Part III. You will take your personal research and notes and participate in a Socratic "Storyboard meeting" with your peers to highlight the best approach to accurately identify and retell the story.

Part IV. You will create your own animation and assemble your movie to meet the following requirements that focus on Exodus 1-20.

Elements Needed (Minimum of 3-5 slides and references for each section of the story.

- Introduction,
- Act I, Life and Character of Moses,
- Act II. Moses, Pharaoh, Idolatry, Plagues,
- Act III. The Passover,
- Conclusion

Passover Project Rubric

	Below Standard	Approaching Standard	At Standard	Above Standard
Explanation of Ideas, Information and Content	• Too few, inappropriate or irrelevant descriptions, facts, details or examples to clearly explain ideas or content	• Uses some descriptions, facts and details but some may be irrelevant or there may still be an inadequate amount	• Uses relevant, well-chosen descriptions, facts, details and examples to support claims and to address the Driving Question	
Organization and Clarity	• Does not address driving question or include require content in the presentation • Does not organize content in a manner that provides clarity or makes sense • Does not have an introduction or conclusion • The presentation is too short and does not represent effort or interaction.	• Includes nearly all criteria outlined in the Driving Question or presentation rubric • Some content is organized and makes sense but other parts seem out of order or lack organization • Introduction and conclusion exist but do not add value to the presentation • Overall presentation is within limits but may spend too much or too little time on an idea or visual aid	• Includes all criteria outlined in the Driving Question or presentation rubric • Moves clearly through the presentation with ideas and concepts building naturally • Introduction and conclusion is effective • Time is well organized and presentation is not rushed or long	
Visual Aids	• Does not use audio or visual aids or media • Visual or Media is distracting	• Some visual or media aides are distracting or do not add value to the presentation	• Well produced and created audio/visual aides that clarify information adding value and interest	
Response to Questions	• Does not address audience questions or interact with audience	• Some audience interaction but not always clearly or completely	• Clear and intentional audience interaction • Able to admit when they do not know an answer but can offer a possible solution of where to look	

Character Study. Moses; Man of passion and leader of the people of God

Examine the irony of the life of Moses. A man who stuttered and acted out in anger who would become the spokesperson for and the friend of; God.

What were the beliefs and convictions of Moses? How do you know?

What private thoughts from Moses are revealed to us?

What are the actions or events from the life of Moses that shaped him into the man he was and the one he would become?

How would you describe the character of Moses (be sure to answer why and explain your response with references).

What does the life of Moses teach me about second chances?

BELIEFS

What does this reveal to us about God?

VALUES

ACTIONS

What does this reveal to us about myself?

HABITS

Passover: The conflict rises

Passover Project Part I. Watch the movies and identify the elements of the plot and the story.

Setting:
Where:

When:

Major Characters:

Minor Characters:

Plot/Problem:

Event 1:

Event 2:

Event 3:

Outcome:

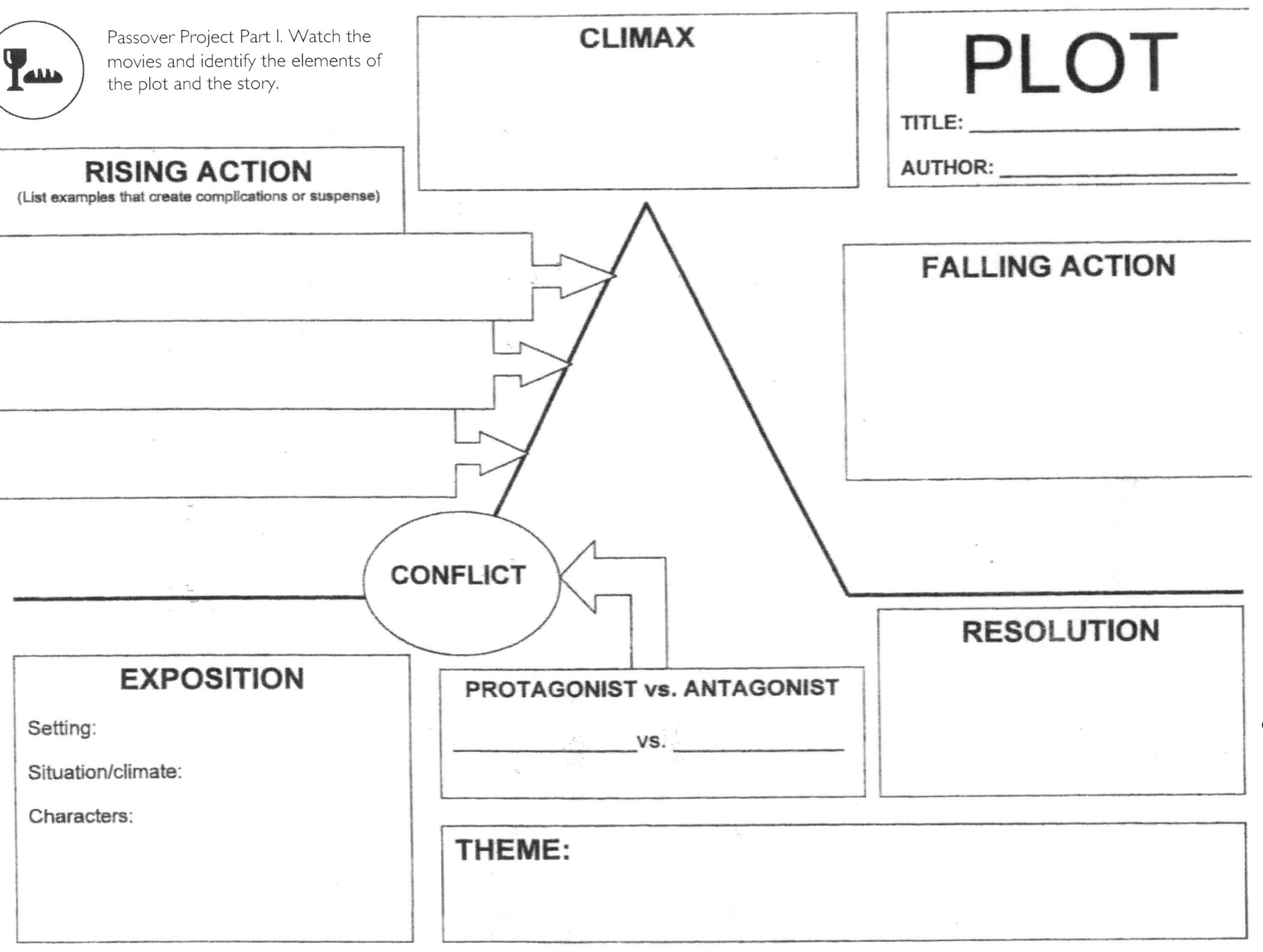
Passover Project Part I. Watch the movies and identify the elements of the plot and the story.
CLIMAX
PLOT
TITLE: ____
AUTHOR: ____
RISING ACTION
(List examples that create complications or suspense)
FALLING ACTION
CONFLICT
RESOLUTION
EXPOSITION
Setting:
Situation/climate:
Characters:
PROTAGONIST vs. ANTAGONIST
____ vs. ____
THEME:

How does God use Egypt to fulfill His mission? Understanding the Context & The Setting

As the sun was setting, Abram fell into a deep sleep, and a thick and dreadful darkness came over him.

Then the Lord said to him, "Know for certain that for four hundred years your descendants will be strangers in a country not their own and that they will be enslaved and mistreated there.

But I will punish the nation they serve as slaves, and afterward they will come out with great possessions.

Genesis 15:12-14

Following the threads...

The Israelites are "fruitful and multiply" and Pharaoh tries to stop them

1. Work them to death – Exodus 1:9-14
2. Kill the newborn boys – Exodus 1:15-21
3. Throw the boys in the Nile – Exodus 1:22

In time, Joseph and all of his brothers died, ending that entire generation. But their descendants, the Israelites, had many children and grandchildren. In fact, they multiplied so greatly that they became extremely powerful and filled the land.

Eventually, a new king came to power in Egypt who knew nothing about Joseph or what he had done. He said to his people, "Look, the people of Israel now outnumber us and are stronger than we are.

We must make a plan to keep them from growing even more. If we don't, and if war breaks out, they will join our enemies and fight against us. Then they will escape from the country."

So the Egyptians made the Israelites their slaves. They appointed brutal slave drivers over them, hoping to wear them down with crushing labor. They forced them to build the cities of Pithom and Rameses as supply centers for the king.

But the more the Egyptians oppressed them, the more the Israelites multiplied and spread, and the more alarmed the Egyptians became.

So the Egyptians worked the people of Israel without mercy.

They made their lives bitter, forcing them to mix mortar **and make bricks** and do all the work in the fields. They were ruthless in all their demands.

Exodus 1:6-14

Want to see something cool?

While the Bible never gives us the exact name of the Pharaoh during the time of the Hebrew Exodus, there are two theories. One theory is that it could have been Ramses II.

If that is the case, then click on the link and get your passport stamped because if you go to Chicago then you can see a Brick in the Chicago Oriental Museum that is made of straw and clay **and** has the signature of Ramses stamped on it.

This is most likely one of the bricks mentioned in Exodus 1.

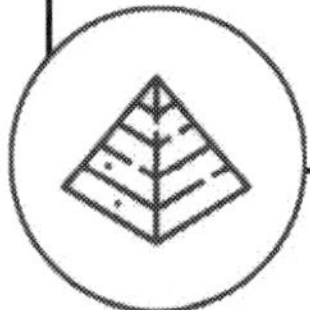

https://www.facebook.com/OrientalInstitute/photos/a.10151241555369486/10157359144139486/?type=3&eid=ARBNVa_jESfMp3G2Lxlz_x2_CLFF9bv4MDUGApp8ZMCCzNFo0uy-Ryl8ql0wftRuWUgbMVbv3EsNFha7&__tn__=EEHH-R

Key Plot Elements & Threads

Key Plot Elements & Threads

Socratic Storyboard

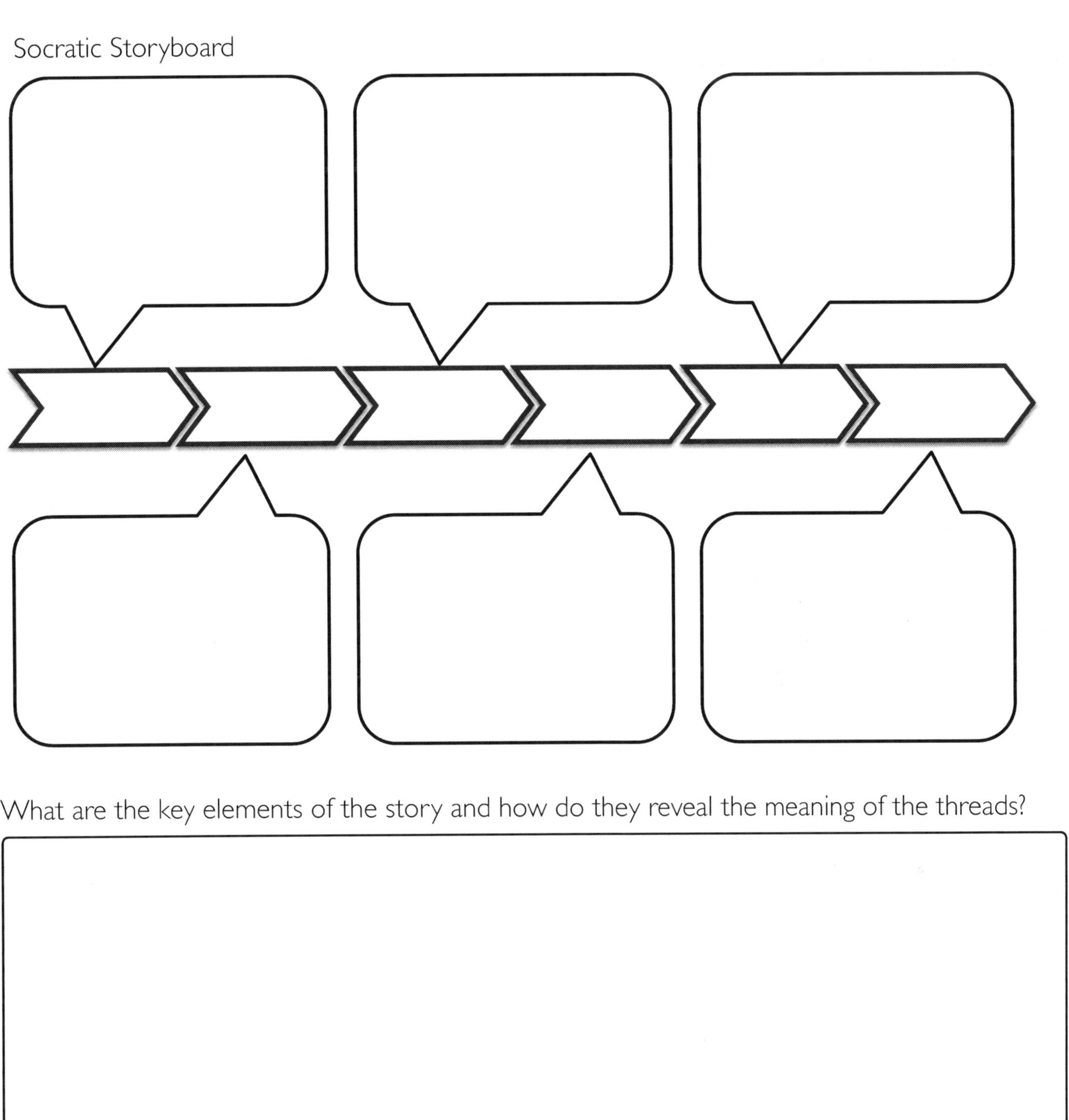

What are the key elements of the story and how do they reveal the meaning of the threads?

Key Plot Points with references.

Introduction,

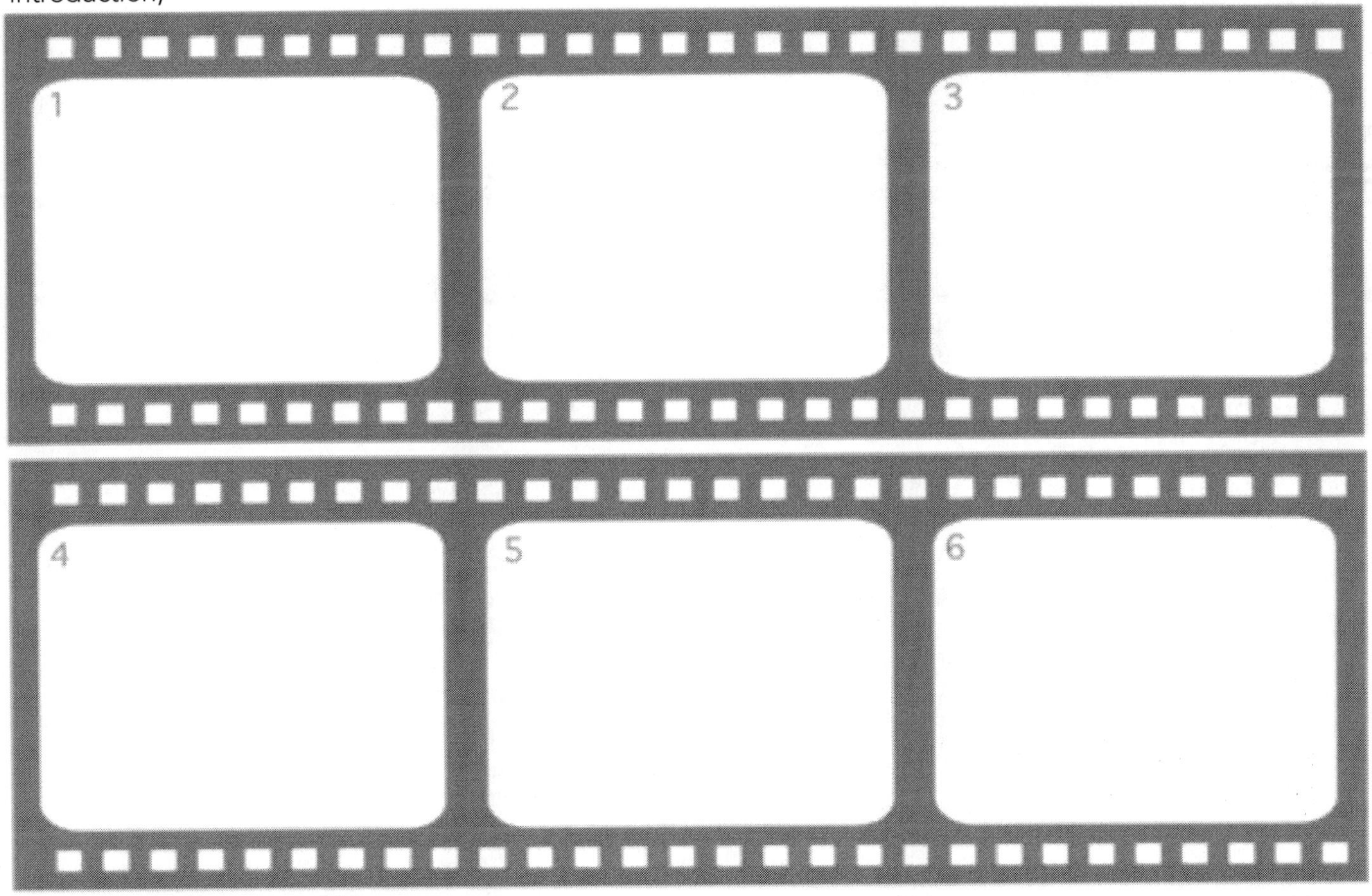

1

2

3

4

5

6

Act I. Life & Character of Moses

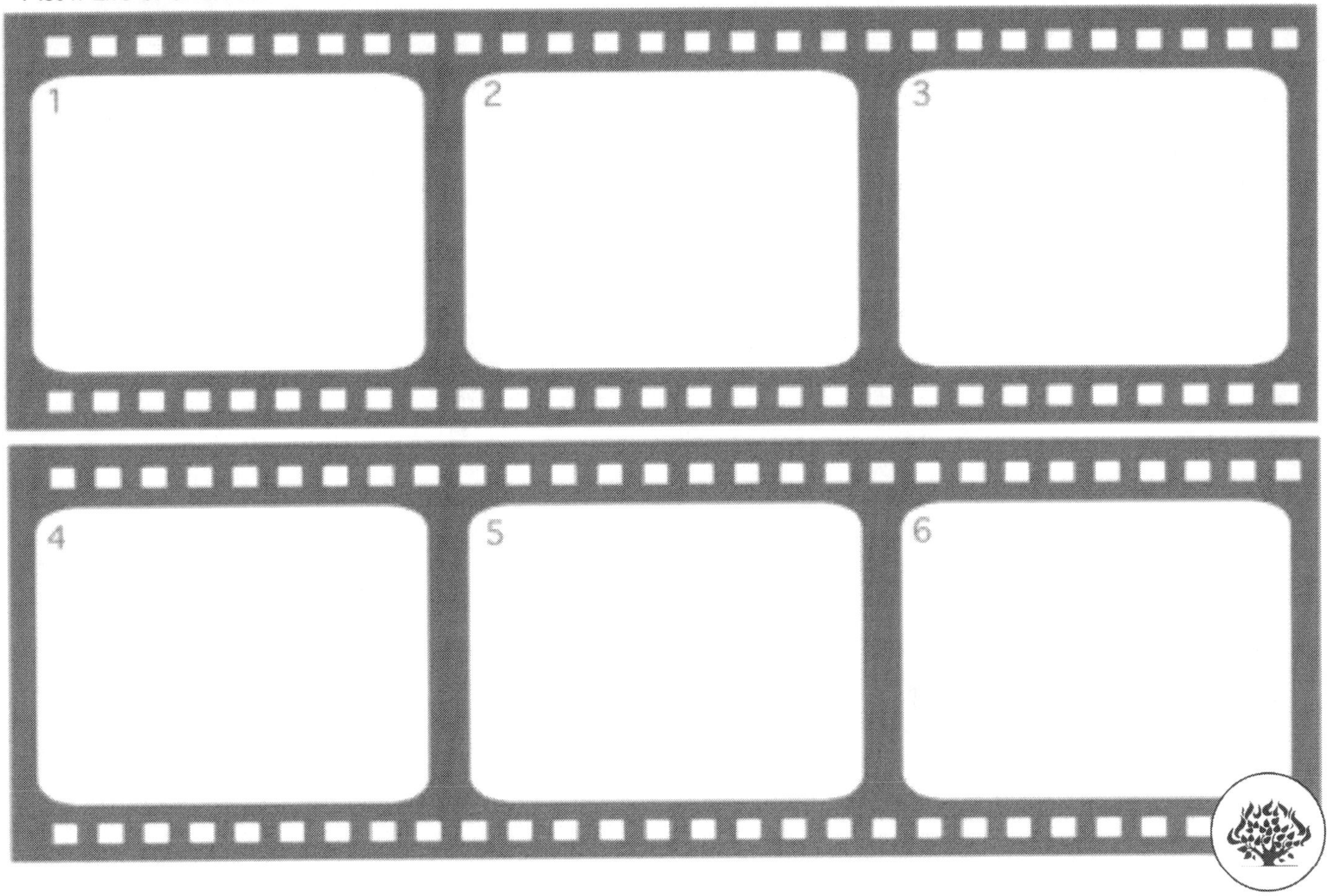

1

2

3

4

5

6

Act II. Pharaoh, Idolatry, Plagues

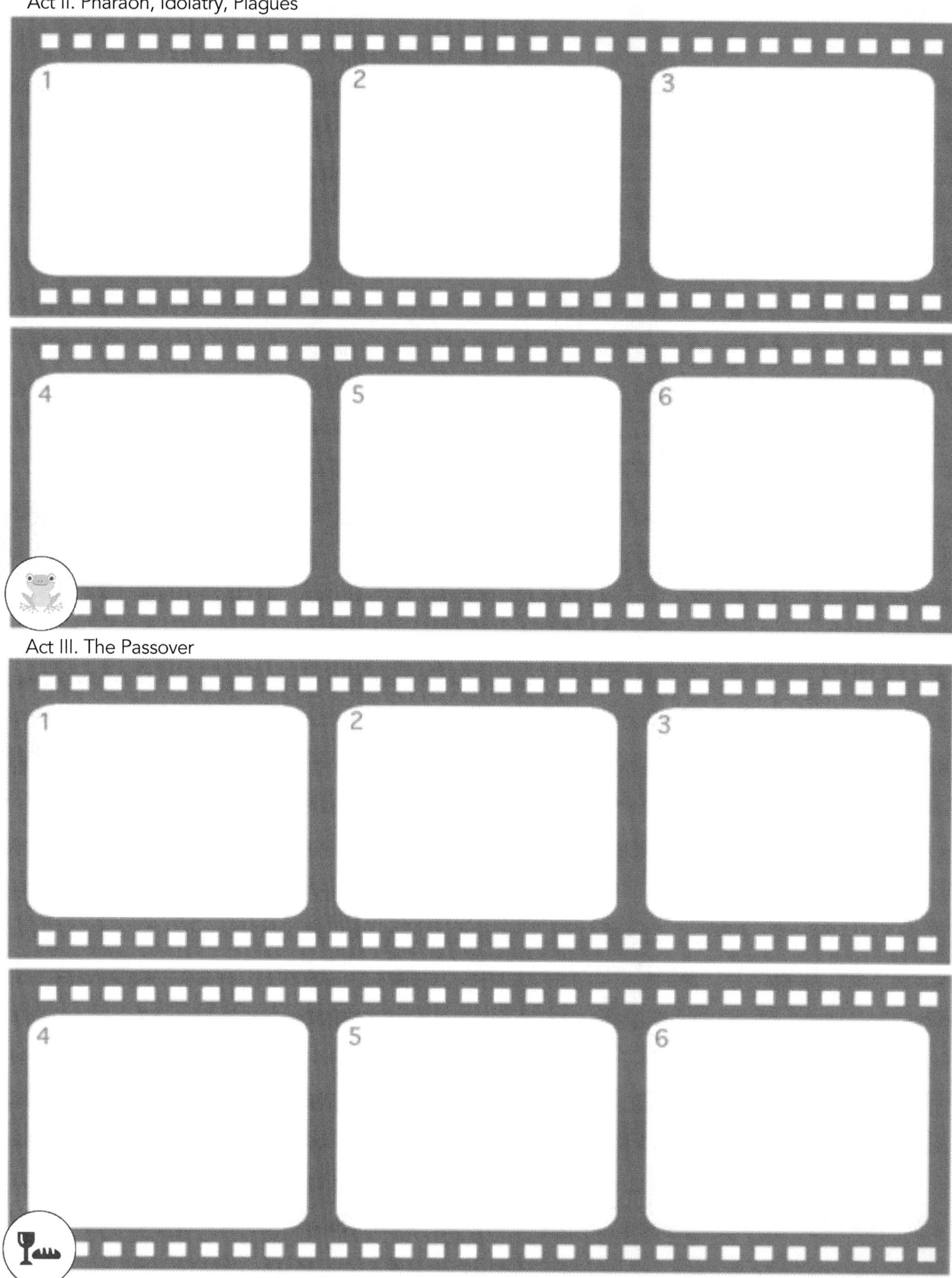

Act III. The Passover

HISTORY

THE MISSION OF GOD

AND THE SECRET OF THE GOLDEN THREAD

pillar

Can God be trusted?

Learning to love God's Word

If you put all these people to death, leaving none alive, the nations who have heard this report about you will say, 'The Lord was not able to bring these people into the land he promised them on oath, so he slaughtered them in the wilderness . . .
The Lord replied, "I have forgiven them, as you asked. Nevertheless, as surely as I live and as surely as the glory of the Lord fills the whole earth, not one of those who saw my glory and the signs I performed in Egypt and in the wilderness but who disobeyed me and tested me ten times not one of them will ever see the land I promised...

Numbers 14:15-16, 20-23a

What is the learning goal for Pillar?

By day the Lord went ahead of them in a pillar of cloud to guide them on their way and by night in a pillar of fire to give them light, so that they could travel by day or night. Neither the pillar of cloud by day nor the pillar of fire by night left its place in front of the people.

Exodus 13:21-22

PILLAR

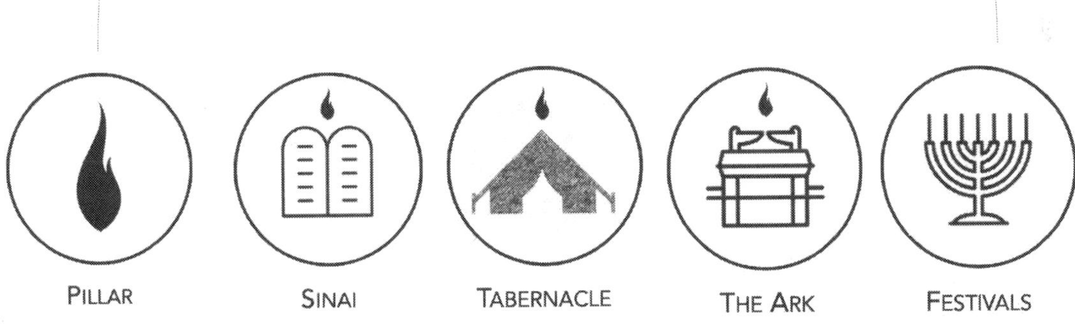

For some of us the idea that Jesus wants to have a "personal relationship with us" is completely foreign.

How could a god, any god, have a desire to have a relationship with a human (any human)?

It almost feels humorous to think about. The idea that an infinite God, who does not need anything, would desire a relationship with a finite human, who needs everything… seems odd.

But that is one of the main themes of this section of His Story. It is the section of the story where God reintroduces Himself to His people and invites them to enjoy and find confidence in His presence and power.

After 400 years in slavery in the land of Egypt, God provided the deliverer Moses to lead His people out of the land of slavery and into the land of promise.

God begins this section of His story with a plan to graciously reintroduce Himself to a people who had become accustomed to idolatry.

His desire was to bless the people and to provide them with time to grow in their relationship with Him and the opportunity to remove idolatrous habits that had contaminated their way of life before leading them into the land of Promise.

Central to this section of His Story is the reminder that God desires to be known and to have a relationship with us and to "make tabernacle" with us as time and time again Israel finds themselves in His presence.

Pillar; The Presence, Power and Holiness of God

Setting:
Where:

When:

Major Characters:

Minor Characters:

Plot/Problem:

Event 1:

Event 2:

Event 3:

Outcome:

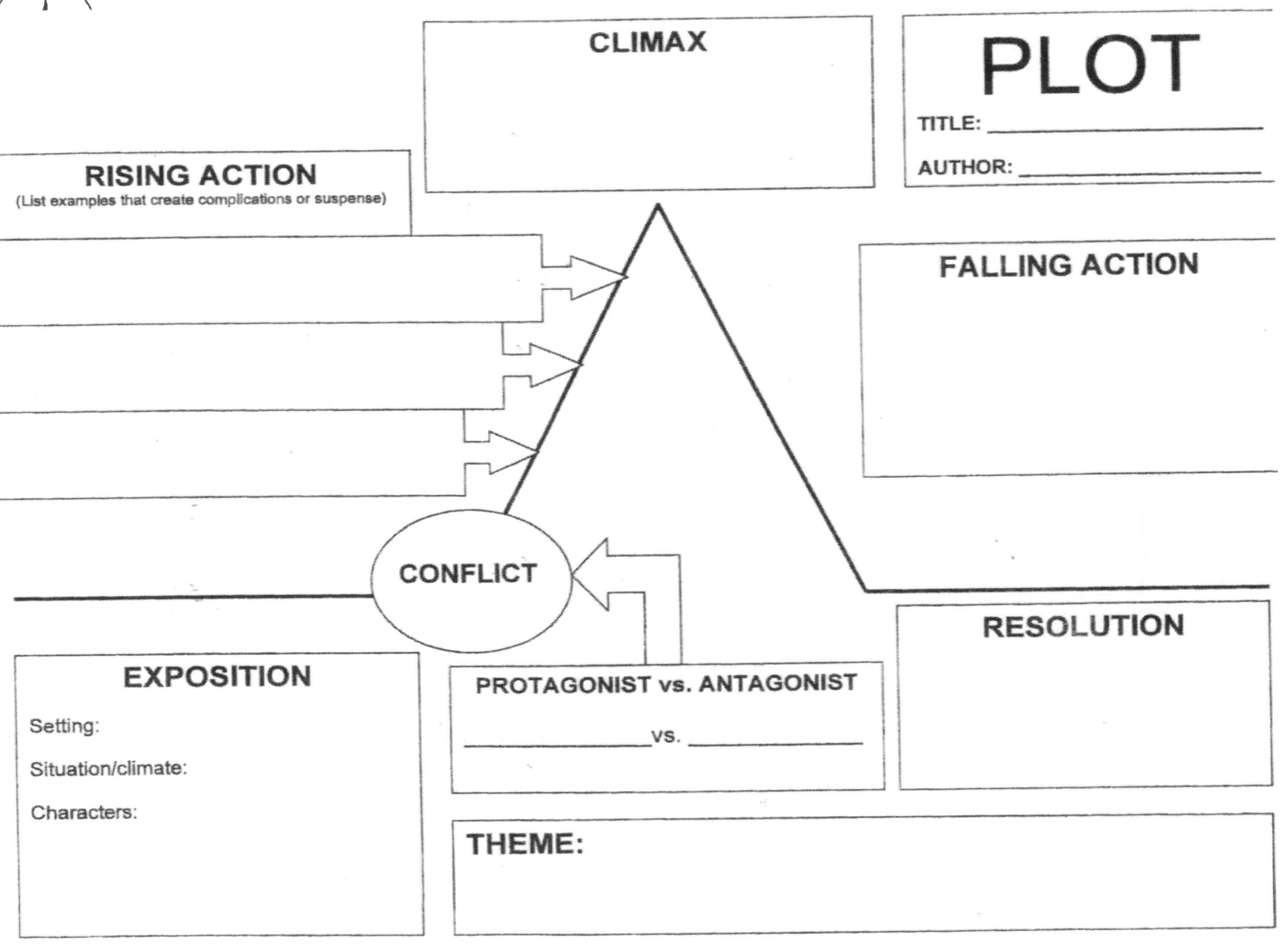
CLIMAX
PLOT
TITLE:
AUTHOR:
RISING ACTION
(List examples that create complications or suspense)
FALLING ACTION
CONFLICT
RESOLUTION
EXPOSITION
Setting:
Situation/climate:
Characters:
PROTAGONIST vs. ANTAGONIST
vs.
THEME:

Exodus 13. Is God efficient?

[17] When Pharaoh finally let the people go, God did not lead them along the main road that runs through Philistine territory, **even though that was the shortest route** to the Promised Land. God said, "If the people are faced with a battle, they might change their minds and return to Egypt." **18** So God led them in a roundabout way through the wilderness toward the Red Sea. Thus the Israelites left Egypt like an army ready for battle.

19 Moses took the bones of Joseph with him, for Joseph had made the sons of Israel swear to do this. He said, "God will certainly come to help you. When he does, you must take my bones with you from this place."

20 The Israelites left Succoth and camped at Etham on the edge of the wilderness. **21** The Lord went ahead of them. He guided them during the day with a pillar of cloud, and he provided light at night with a pillar of fire. This allowed them to travel by day or by night. **22** And the Lord did not remove the pillar of cloud or pillar of fire from its place in front of the people.

Exodus 13:17-22

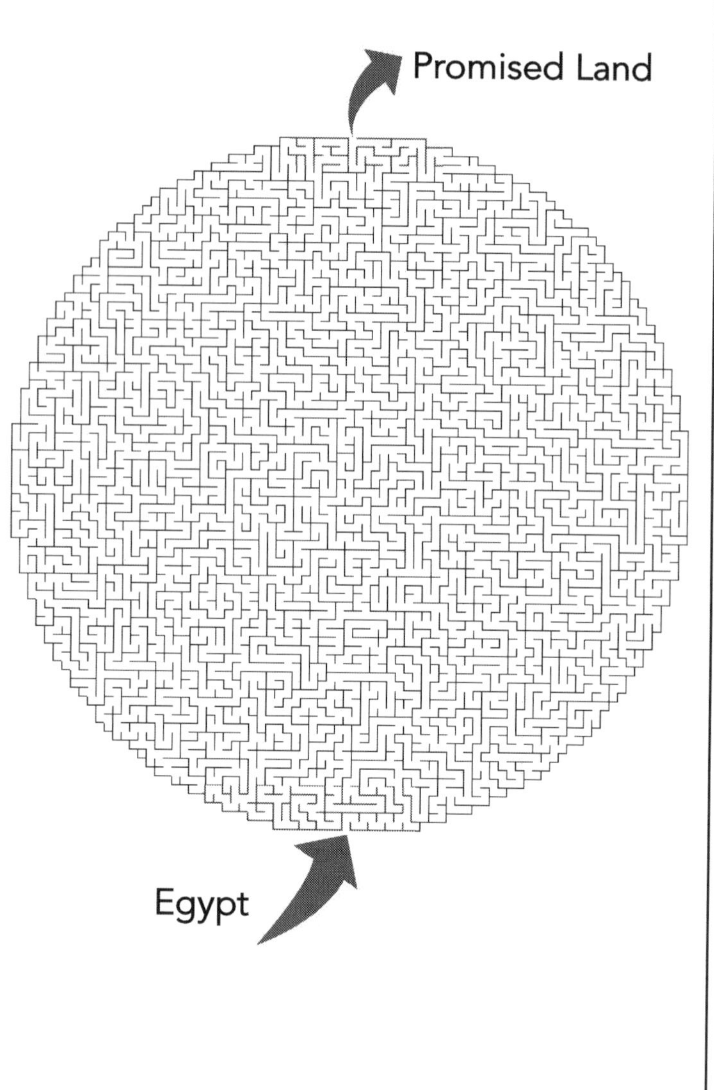

Examine this passage and identify all of the very unique but intentional ways that God was demonstrating His love to the children of Israel.

Define the Terms

What does it mean to be **efficient**?

What does it mean to be **sufficient**?

Explain the statement, God is sufficient but He is not efficient.

Where are some places in my life where God has not been efficient?

How have I responded to Him?

BELIEFS

How will I respond? Why?

VALUES

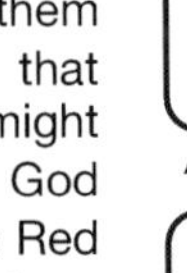

ACTIONS

HABITS

[17] When Pharaoh let the people go, God did not lead them on the road through the Philistine country, though that was shorter. For God said, "If they face war, they might change their minds and return to Egypt." [18] So God led the people around by the desert road toward the Red Sea. The Israelites went up out of Egypt ready for battle.
Exodus 13:17-18

A Kingdom of Priests

On the first day of the third month after the
Israelites left Egypt—on that very day—they
came to the Desert of Sinai. 2 After they set
out from Rephidim, they entered the Desert of
Sinai, and Israel camped there in the desert in
front of the mountain.
3 Then Moses went up to God, and
the Lord called to him from the mountain and
said, "This is what you are to say to the
descendants of Jacob and what you are to tell
the people of Israel: 4 'You yourselves have
seen what I did to Egypt, and how I carried
you on eagles' wings and brought you to
myself. 5 Now if you obey me fully and keep
my covenant, then out of all nations you will
be my treasured possession. Although the
whole earth is mine, 6 you will be for me a
kingdom of priests and a holy nation.' These
are the words you are to speak to the
Israelites."
7 So Moses went back and summoned the
elders of the people and set before them all
the words the Lord had commanded him to
speak. 8 The people all responded together,
"We will do everything the Lord has said." So
Moses brought their answer back to the Lord.
9 The Lord said to Moses, "I am going to come
to you in a dense cloud, so that the people
will hear me speaking with you and will always
put their trust in you." Then Moses told
the Lord what the people had said.
10 And the Lord said to Moses, "Go to the
people and consecrate them today and
tomorrow. Have them wash their
clothes 11 and be ready by the third
day, because on that day the Lord will come
down on Mount Sinai in the sight of all the
people. 12 Put limits for the people around the
mountain and tell them, 'Be careful that you
do not approach the mountain or touch the
foot of it. Whoever touches the mountain is to
be put to death. 13 They are to be stoned or
shot with arrows; not a hand is to be laid on
them. No person or animal shall be permitted
to live.' Only when the ram's horn sounds a
long blast may they approach the mountain."

16 On the morning of the third day there was
thunder and lightning, with a thick cloud over
the mountain, and a very loud trumpet
blast. Everyone in the camp trembled. 17 Then
Moses led the people out of the camp to
meet with God, and they stood at the foot of
the mountain. 18 Mount Sinai was covered with
smoke, because the Lord descended on it in
fire. The smoke billowed up from it like smoke
from a furnace, and the whole mountain
trembled violently. 19 As the sound of the
trumpet grew louder and louder, Moses spoke
and the voice of God answered him.

and He has made us to be a kingdom, priests to His God and Father--to Him be the glory and the dominion forever and ever. Amen.

Revelation 1:6

But you are a chosen race, a royal priesthood, a Holy Nation, A people for God's own possession, **so that you may proclaim the excellencies of Him who has called** you out of darkness into His marvelous light;

1 Peter 2:9

you also, as living stones, are being built up as a spiritual house for **a holy priesthood, to offer up spiritual sacrifices** acceptable to God through Jesus Christ.

1 Peter 2:5

The Presence, Power and Holiness of God

By day the Lord went ahead of them in a pillar of cloud to guide them on their way and by night in a pillar of fire to give them light, so that they could travel by day or night. Neither the pillar of cloud by day nor the pillar of fire by night left its place in front of the people. Exodus 13:21-22

How different is our relationship to God from that of Old Testament Israel?

At Sinai, the people trembled at God's presence and were afraid to be near Him (Exodus 19:16). What is my response to the invitation to be the presence of God? Why What influences my response?

How do I practice the presence of God in my life?

Beliefs

Values

Actions

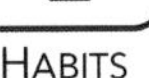

Habits

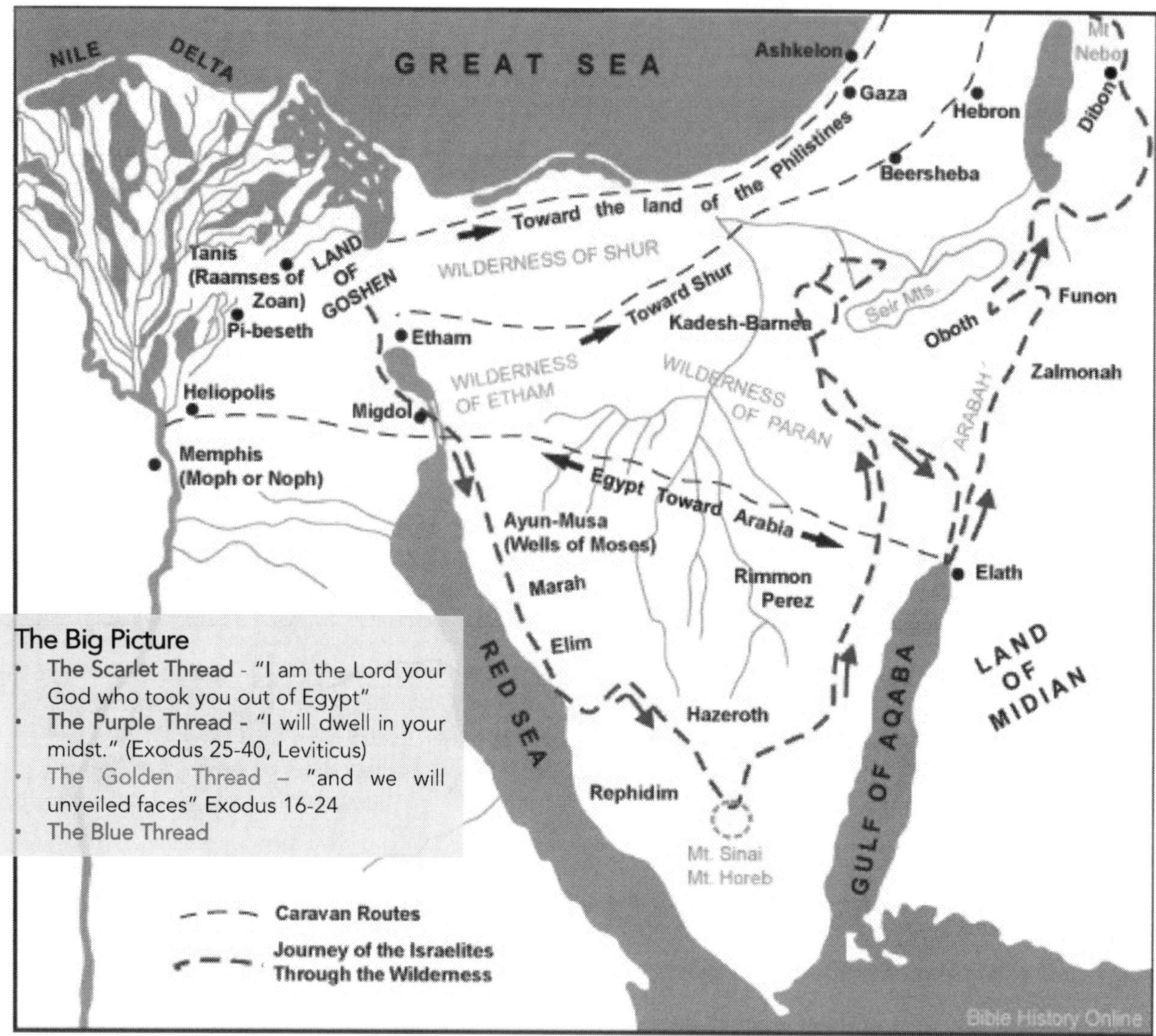

The Big Picture

- The Scarlet Thread - "I am the Lord your God who took you out of Egypt"
- The Purple Thread - "I will dwell in your midst." (Exodus 25-40, Leviticus)
- The Golden Thread – "and we will unveiled faces" Exodus 16-24
- The Blue Thread

How did God deliver the Israelites out of Egypt? (Exodus 12:33-41; 13:17-31)

How did the Israelites fail to acknowledge God's provision?

How did the Israelites respond to their hardships? Grumbling and complaining

- At the Red Sea (Exodus 14:11-12)
- At Marah (Exodus 15:24)
- In the Wilderness of Sin (Exodus 16:2-3)
- At Meribah (Exodus 17:2)
- At Mt. Sinai – Golden Calf (Exodus 32:1-10)

How should we respond to hardships in our lives? (Philippians 2:14-16; James 1:2-4)

Sinai. The Presence, Power and Holiness of God

430 years have passed. God is reintroducing himself to his people.

How does the introduction of Gods law position his people for his purpose?

How is the pillar and the cloud symbolic of the sacred space of the kingdom of God in the midst of the wilderness?

Exodus 31:1-28

32 When the people saw how long it was taking Moses to come back down the mountain, they gathered around Aaron. "Come on," they said, "make us some gods who can lead us. We don't know what happened to this fellow Moses, who brought us here from the land of Egypt."

2 So Aaron said, "Take the gold rings from the ears of your wives and sons and daughters, and bring them to me."

3 All the people took the gold rings from their ears and brought them to Aaron. 4 Then Aaron took the gold, melted it down, and molded it into the shape of a calf. When the people saw it, they exclaimed, "O Israel, these are the gods who brought you out of the land of Egypt!"

5 Aaron saw how excited the people were, so he built an altar in front of the calf. Then he announced, "Tomorrow will be a festival to the Lord!"

6 The people got up early the next morning to sacrifice burnt offerings and peace offerings. After this, they celebrated with feasting and drinking, and they indulged in pagan revelry.

7 The Lord told Moses, "Quick! Go down the mountain! Your people whom you brought from the land of Egypt have corrupted themselves. 8 How quickly they have turned away from the way I commanded them to live! They have melted down gold and made a calf, and they have bowed down and sacrificed to it. They are saying, 'These are your gods, O Israel, who brought you out of the land of Egypt.'"

9 Then the Lord said, "I have seen how stubborn and rebellious these people are. 10 Now leave me alone so my fierce anger can blaze against them, and I will destroy them. Then I will make you, Moses, into a great nation."

11 But Moses tried to pacify the Lord his God. "O Lord!" he said. "Why are you so angry with your own people whom you brought from the land of Egypt with such great power and such a strong hand? 12 Why let the Egyptians say, 'Their God rescued them with the evil intention of slaughtering them in the mountains and wiping them from the face of the earth'? Turn away from your fierce anger. Change your mind about this terrible disaster you have threatened against your people!

13 Remember your servants Abraham, Isaac, and Jacob. You bound yourself with an oath to them, saying, 'I will make your descendants as numerous as the stars of heaven. And I will give them all of this land that I have promised to your descendants, and they will possess it forever.'"

14 So the Lord changed his mind about the terrible disaster he had threatened to bring on his people.

15 Then Moses turned and went down the mountain. He held in his hands the two stone tablets inscribed with the terms of the covenant.[b] They were inscribed on both sides, front and back. 16 These tablets were God's work; the words on them were written by God himself.

17 When Joshua heard the boisterous noise of the people shouting below them, he exclaimed to Moses, "It sounds like war in the camp!"

18 But Moses replied, "No, it's not a shout of victory nor the wailing of defeat. I hear the sound of a celebration."

19 When they came near the camp, Moses saw the calf and the dancing, and he burned with anger. He threw the stone tablets to the ground, smashing them at the foot of the mountain. 20 He took the calf they had made and burned it. Then he ground it into powder, threw it into the water, and forced the people to drink it.

21 Finally, he turned to Aaron and demanded, "What did these people do to you to make you bring such terrible sin upon them?"

22 "Don't get so upset, my lord," Aaron replied. "You yourself know how evil these people are. 23 They said to me, 'Make us gods who will lead us. We don't know what happened to this fellow Moses, who brought us here from the land of Egypt.' 24 So I told them, 'Whoever has gold jewelry, take it off.' When they brought it to me, I simply threw it into the fire—and out came this calf!"

25 Moses saw that Aaron had let the people get completely out of control, much to the amusement of their enemies.[c] 26 So he stood at the entrance to the camp and shouted, "All of you who are on the Lord's side, come here and join me." And all the Levites gathered around him.

27 Moses told them, "This is what the Lord, the God of Israel, says: Each of you, take your swords and go back and forth from one end of the camp to the other. Kill everyone—even your brothers, friends, and neighbors." 28 The Levites obeyed Moses' command, and about 3,000 people died that day.

The elements of the Tabernacle

How do I approach the presence of God?

The pieces of furniture were thoughtfully placed in the structure. As the priests approached each piece on a daily basis they demonstrated to all of Israel and us, how God is to be approached.

1. The Entrance Gate

"The curtain that covered the entrance to the courtyard was made of fine linen cloth and embroidered with **blue, purple, and scarlet yarn**.

"It was 30 feet long and 7 1/2 feet high, just like the curtains of the courtyard walls."

Exodus 38:9-20

The colors are significant: blue (the Word of God- prophet), red (The Redemption of God - priest), and purple (The Kingdom of God - king).

Jesus fulfills all three threads and all three offices.

He is the gate: "Yes, I am the gate. Those who come in through me will be saved. Wherever they go, they will find green pastures."

John 10:9

If we want to approach God and have a relationship with Him, we come through Jesus.

2. The Bronze Altar

"Using acacia wood, make a square altar 7 1/2 feet wide, 7 1/2 feet long, and 4 1/2 feet high."

Exodus 27:1-8

Every morning and evening, animals were sacrificed on the altar. Sheep or oxen were sacrificed in our place, which provided entry to God's presence. This all points towards Jesus who would die on the Cross 1,400 years in the future:

"Behold! The Lamb of God who takes away the sin of the world!"

John 1:29

3. The Bronze Basin (laver)

"Make a large bronze wash basin with a bronze pedestal. Put it between the Tabernacle and the altar, and fill it with water."

Exodus. 30:17-21

Here the priests would wash their hands and feet before entering the Holy Place. The substitution of Christ's blood on the cross and the resurrection of Christ from the dead cleanses us from the stain of sin

"And so, dear brothers and sisters, we can boldly enter heaven's Most Holy Place because of the blood of Jesus." Heb. 10:19

Second Symbol: The water is an illustration of baptism and the outward symbol of the inward renewal and and transformation to enter into the presence of a Holy God.

4. The Table of Bread

"Then make a table of acacia wood, 3 feet long, 1 1/2 feet wide, and 2 1/4 feet high… You must always keep the special Bread of the Presence on the table before me."

Exodus. 25:23-30

The first item in the Holy Place: Twelve loaves of bread = placed on the table every day to remind the people that God would provide for their daily needs. (*Give us this day our daily bread*).

"I am the bread of life. He who comes to Me shall never hunger, and he who believes in Me shall never thirst."

John 6:35

"Man shall not live by bread alone, but by every word that proceeds from the mouth of God."

Matthew. 4:4

A reminder of our need to feed on the Word every day – it is food and nourishment for our spirits.

5. The Golden Lampstand (menorah)

"You shall also make a lampstand of pure gold; the lampstand shall be of hammered work. Its shaft, its branches, its bowls, its ornamental knobs, and flowers shall be of one piece... You shall make seven lamps for it, and they shall arrange its lamps so that they give light in front of it."

Exodus 25:31-40

Jesus said, "I am the light of the world. He who follows Me shall not walk in darkness, but have the light of life."

John 8:12

The Holy Spirit: Throughout all of Scripture oil is a symbol of the Holy Spirit.

The Word of God: "Your word is a lamp to my feet And a light to my path." Psalm 119:105

Reflection: Of the six side candlesticks, they each have nine almond blossoms (6 x 9 = 54).

- On the middle candlestick, there are 12 blossoms (54 + 12 = 66).
- The total of the first four candlesticks = 39;
- The total of the last three candlesticks = 27.

6. The Altar of Incense

"Then make a small altar out of acacia wood for burning incense."

Exodus 30:1-10

This altar stood right outside of the doorway to the Most Holy Place (Holiest of Holies). Throughout Scripture pure worship of God is referenced as "a fragrant offering that is pleasing to Him."

The fragrance of the incense is a reminder that before we can enter into the presence of God we must come before Him with the fragrance of pure worship.

Between the Holy Place and the Most Holy Place was a four-inch-thick Veil. Only the High Priest entered there once a year on The Day of Atonement.

When Jesus died on the Cross hundreds of years later, the Veil was torn in two, symbolically revealing to us that we have continuous access to the presence of God.

7. The Ark of The Covenant

"And they shall make an ark of acacia wood... And there I will meet with you, and I will speak with you from above the mercy seat, from between the two cherubim which are on the ark of the Testimony, about everything which I will give you in commandment to the children of Israel."

Exodus 25:10-22)

There was only one piece of furniture in the Most Holy Place: The Ark. This was the place where God promised to meet with the High Priest.

Hebrews paints a beautiful picture of how Jesus is the fulfillment of the Tabernacle.

"Let us, therefore, come boldly to the throne of grace, that we may obtain mercy and find grace to help in time of need." Hebrews. 4:16

THE TABERNACLE OF MOSES (EXODUS 35-40)

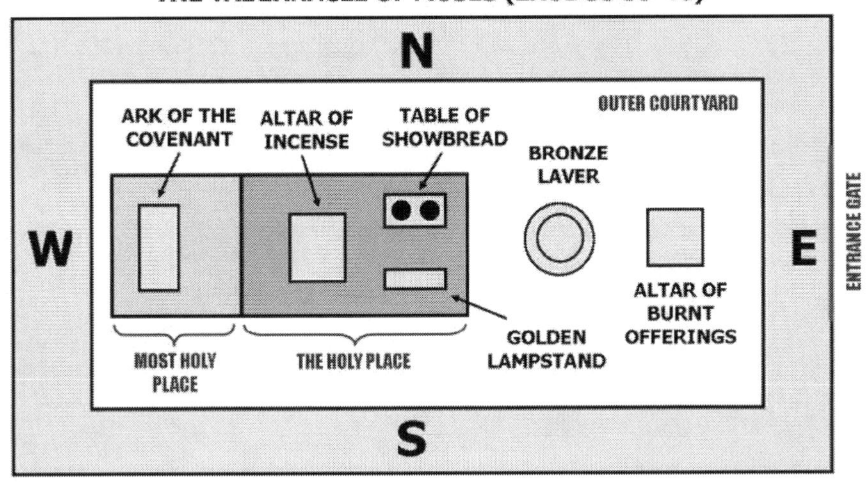

The Tabernacle & The Threads

1. Reflect God's mission (The Golden Thread of God's Glory)

The earth is filled with the glory of God through his creation (Isaiah 6:3), but his desire from the beginning was to fill the earth with his glory in a special way by partnering with mankind (Genesis 1:28). People bear God's Image in this world uniquely. The first people walked with God in uninterrupted fellowship in the Garden.

When mankind sinned and fell away from God, his presence was removed from the earth too. Mankind was unable to fulfill his mission to fill the earth with God's glory without the presence of God with them (Genesis 1-11). After our ancient ancestors were escorted out of Eden and God's presence, he remained distant from humanity and worked through mediators like Noah, Abraham, and Moses alone. However, he desired to be amongst his people, like he was with Adam.

God chooses Abraham and his descendants to fulfill the promise given to Eve to crush the kingdom of darkness and to fill the earth with his glory (Genesis 12). He then uses the imagery of the Garden and the venue of first the Tabernacle and then the Temple to intentionally be among the children of Israel.

2. Designed to bring people back to the Garden (The Purple Thread of God's presence)

The Tabernacle was the place where God would dwell with his people since the Garden of Eden. He would be manifest to the Israelites through fire by night and cloud by day. Everyone could see that God was with them.

This is the Tent of Meeting where God was present with Israel. God wanted the place where he met with his people to be special and reflect the original Garden.

What helps us see the parallels between the Garden of Eden and the Tabernacle is the fact that many of the artistic implements and decor within the tent reflect the Garden. The Gold, bdellium, onyx, almond tree, and pomegranate figures, etc.... used in the Tabernacle are not only Eden imagery but are taken from the region where Eden supposedly was located. These artistic artifacts were echoing back to the days when God and man walked together in shameless splendor.

So, God placing his Spirit upon the craftsman doing much of this symbolic labor makes total sense. God's Spirit comes upon important people at important times in the Old Testament to reveal and accomplish his divine will. His desire to dwell among men is wonderfully on display when the Spirit comes upon Bezalel to adorn the Tabernacle of his presence. The beauty and perfection of his work mattered - symbolizing the glory of the Lord at the center of the Israelite camp and the bringing of heaven and earth together again.

3. Reflect God's promise (The Scarlet Thread of God's redemption)

The book of Exodus ends with the Tabernacle built to house God's presence amongst the people, but Moses could not enter.

Why? Because of the sins of the people.

The next book in the OT reveals the temporary solution to the problem. Leviticus outlines the sacrificial system where the lifeblood of animals temporarily covered over the sins of the priest and the people.

The Presence of God in the midst of the people

This tabernacle sat in the center of the Israelite wilderness camp. The camp was divided with the various tribes on each side of the tabernacle. The huge tribe of Judah numbering 186,400 men was the biggest, and faced the door on the east. The smallest tribe of Ephraim, Manasseh and Benjamin had 108,100 and faced the west. On the south was the encampment of Rueben, Simeon and Gad, under the standard of Reuben, numbering 151,450 men. To the north was Dan, accompanied by Asher and Naphtali, making another 157,600 men…

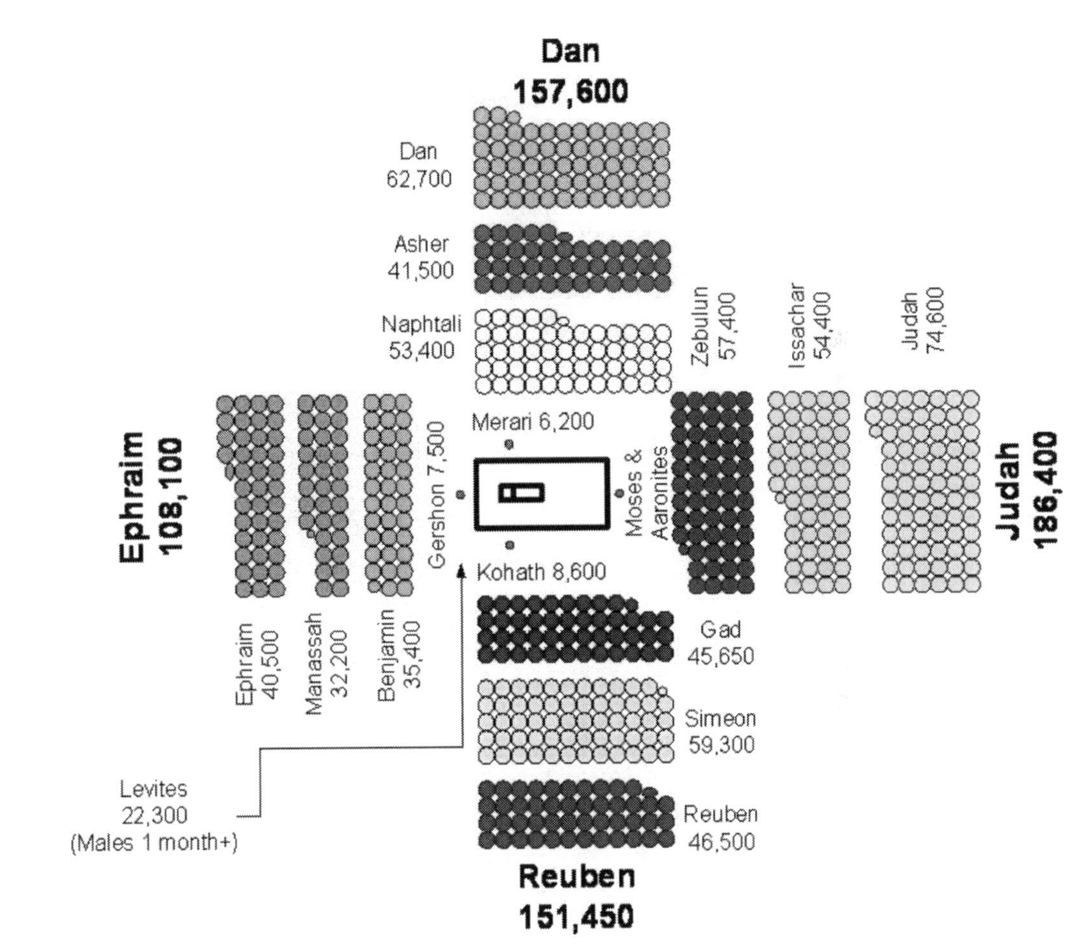

"How beautiful are your tents, O Jacob, your dwelling places, O Israel!"
Numbers 24:5

The Cloud Above the Tabernacle

34 Then the cloud covered the tent of
meeting, and the glory of the Lord filled
the tabernacle. 35 Moses could not enter
the tent of meeting because the cloud had
settled on it, and the glory of
the Lord filled the tabernacle.

36 In all the travels of the Israelites,
whenever the cloud lifted from above the
tabernacle, they would set out; 37 but if the
cloud did not lift, they did not set out—
until the day it lifted.

38 So the cloud of the Lord was over the
tabernacle by day, and fire was in the
cloud by night, in the sight of all the
Israelites during all their travels.

Exodus 40:34-38

15 On the day the tabernacle, the tent of the
covenant law, was set up, the cloud covered it. From
evening till morning the cloud above the tabernacle
looked like fire. 16 That is how it continued to be; the
cloud covered it, and at night it looked like fire. 1

7 Whenever the cloud lifted from above the tent, the
Israelites set out; wherever the cloud settled, the
Israelites encamped. 18 At the Lord's command the
Israelites set out, and at his command they
encamped. As long as the cloud stayed over the
tabernacle, they remained in camp.

19 When the cloud remained over the tabernacle a
long time, the Israelites obeyed the Lord's order and
did not set out. 20 Sometimes the cloud was over the
tabernacle only a few days; at the Lord's command
they would encamp, and then at his command they
would set out.
21 Sometimes the cloud stayed only from evening till
morning, and when it lifted in the morning, they set
out. Whether by day or by night, whenever the cloud
lifted, they set out. 22 Whether the cloud stayed over
the tabernacle for two days or a month or a year, the
Israelites would remain in camp and not set out; but
when it lifted, they would set out.

23 At the Lord's command they encamped, and at
the Lord's command they set out. They obeyed
the Lord's order, in accordance with his command
through Moses.

Numbers 9:15-23

Focus, Faith, Fear

The Lord said to Moses, [2] "Send some men to explore the land of Canaan, which I am giving to the Israelites. From each ancestral tribe send one of its leaders."

Numbers 13:1-2

When Moses sent them to explore Canaan, he said, "Go up through the Negev and on into
the hill country. [18] See what the land is like and whether the people who live there are strong or weak, few or many.

[19] What kind of land do they live in?

Is it good or bad?

What kind of towns do they live in?

Are they unwalled or fortified? [20]

How is the soil? Is it fertile or poor?

Are there trees in it or not?

Do your best to bring back some of the fruit of the land." (It was the season for the first ripe grapes.)

Numbers 13:17-20

At the end of forty days they returned from exploring the land.

Numbers 13:25

26They came back to Moses and Aaron and the whole Israelite community at Kadesh in the Desert of Paran. There they reported to them and to the whole assembly and showed them the fruit of the land.

[27] They gave Moses this account: "We went into the land to which you sent us, and it does flow with milk and honey! Here is its fruit.

[28] But the people who live there are powerful, and the cities are fortified and very large. We even
saw descendants of Anakthere. [29] The
Amalekites live in the Negev; the Hittites, Jebusites and Amoriteslive in the hill country; and the Canaanites live near the sea and along the Jordan."

[30] Then Caleb silenced the people before Moses and said, "We should go up and take possession of the land, for we can certainly do it."

[31] But the men who had gone up with him said, "We can't attack those people; they are stronger
than we are." [32] And they spread among the Israelites a bad report about the land they had explored. They said, "The land we explored devours those living in it. All the people we saw there are of great size.

[33] We saw the Nephilim there (the descendants of Anak come from the Nephilim). We seemed like grasshoppers in our own eyes, and we looked the same to them."

Numbers 13:26-33

Numbers 14
The People Rebel

14 That night all the members of the community raised their voices and wept aloud. 2 All the Israelites grumbled against Moses and Aaron, and the whole assembly said to them, "If only we had died in Egypt! Or in this wilderness! 3 Why is the Lord bringing us to this land only to let us fall by the sword? Our wives and children will be taken as plunder. Wouldn't it be better for us to go back to Egypt?" 4 And they said to each other, "We should choose a leader and go back to Egypt."

5 Then Moses and Aaron fell facedown in front of the whole Israelite assembly gathered there. 6 Joshua son of Nun and Caleb son of Jephunneh, who were among those who had explored the land, tore their clothes 7 and said to the entire Israelite assembly, "The land we passed through and explored is exceedingly good. 8 If the Lord is pleased with us, he will lead us into that land, a land flowing with milk and honey, and will give it to us. 9 Only do not rebel against the Lord. And do not be afraid of the people of the land, because we will devour them. Their protection is gone, but the Lord is with us. Do not be afraid of them."

10 But the whole assembly talked about stoning them. Then the glory of the Lord appeared at the tent of meeting to all the Israelites. 11 The Lord said to Moses, "How long will these people treat me with contempt? How long will they refuse to believe in me, in spite of all the signs I have performed among them? 12 I will strike them down with a plague and destroy them, but I will make you into a nation greater and stronger than they."

13 Moses said to the Lord, "Then the Egyptians will hear about it! By your power you brought these people up from among them. 14 And they will tell the inhabitants of this land about it. They have already heard that you, Lord, are with these people and that you, Lord, have been seen face to face, that your cloud stays over them, and that you go before them in a pillar of cloud by day and a pillar of fire by night. .

15 If you put all these people to death, leaving none alive, the nations who have heard this report about you will say, 16 'The Lord was not able to bring these people into the land he promised them on oath, so he slaughtered them in the wilderness.'

17 "Now may the Lord's strength be displayed, just as you have declared: 18 'The Lord is slow to anger, abounding in love and forgiving sin and rebellion. Yet he does not leave the guilty unpunished; he punishes the children for the sin of the parents to the third and fourth generation.' 19 In accordance with your great love, forgive the sin of these people, just as you have pardoned them from the time they left Egypt until now."

20 The Lord replied, "I have forgiven them, as you asked. 21 Nevertheless, as surely as I live and as surely as the glory of the Lord fills the whole earth, 22 not one of those who saw my glory and the signs I performed in Egypt and in the wilderness but who disobeyed me and tested me ten times— 23 not one of them will ever see the land I promised on oath to their ancestors. No one who has treated me with contempt will ever see it. 24 But because my servant Caleb has a different spirit and follows me wholeheartedly, I will bring him into the land he went to, and his descendants will inherit it. 25

HISTORY

THE MISSION OF GOD

AND THE SECRET OF THE GOLDEN THREAD

promised

Can God be trusted?

Learning to love God's Word

"As for the foreigner who does not belong to your people Israel but has come from a distant land because of your great name... when they come and pray toward this temple, then hear from heaven, your dwelling place. Do whatever the foreigner asks of you, so that all the peoples of the earth may know your name and fear you."

...When Solomon finished praying, fire came down from heaven and consumed the burnt offering and the sacrifices, and the glory of the Lord filled the temple. The priests could not enter the temple of the Lord because the glory of the Lord filled it.

2 Chronicles 6:32-33, 7:1-2

What is the learning goal for Promised?

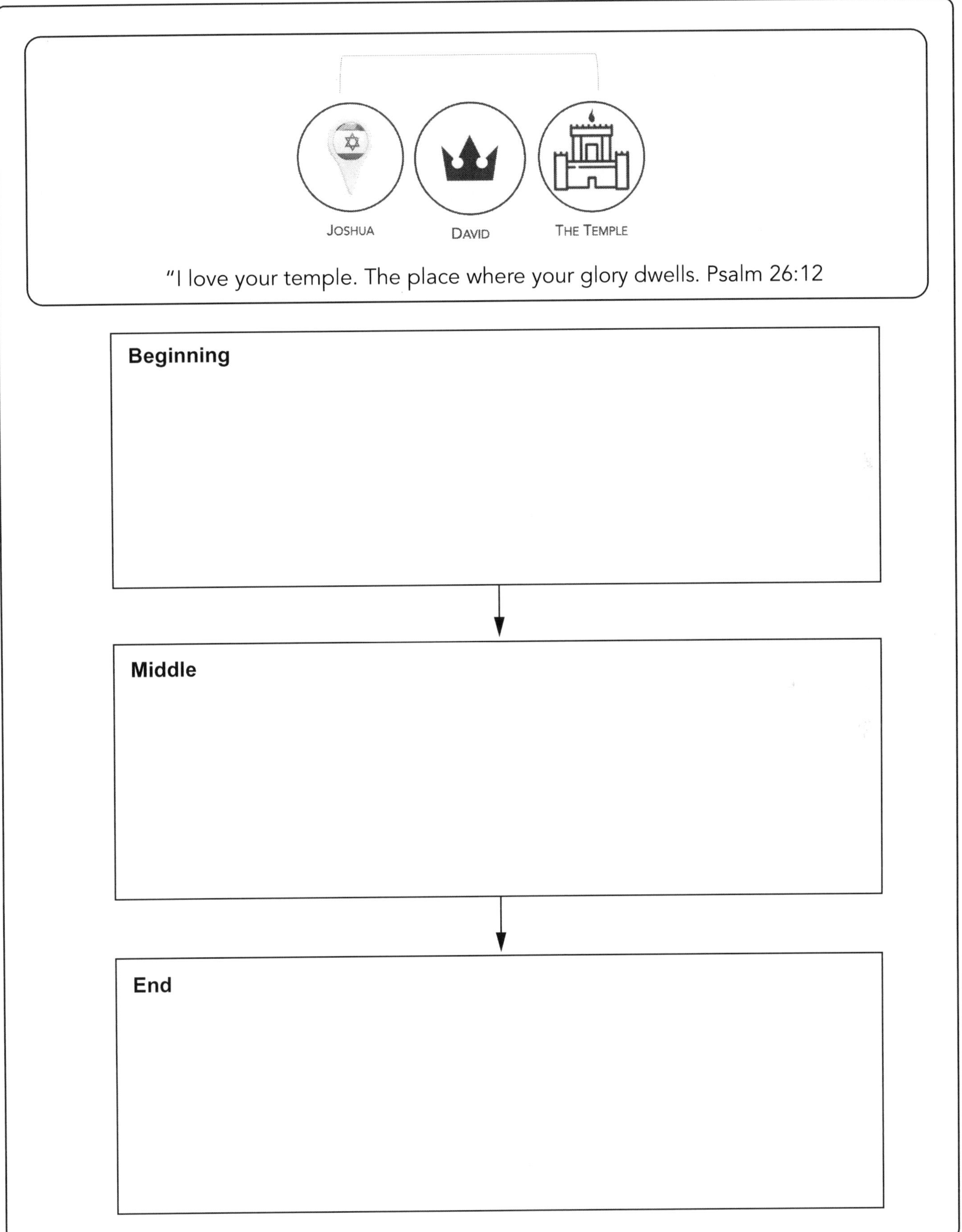

Promise; Mission Accomplished?

Setting:
Where:

When:

Major Characters:

Minor Characters:

Plot/Problem:

Event 1:

Event 2:

Event 3:

Outcome:

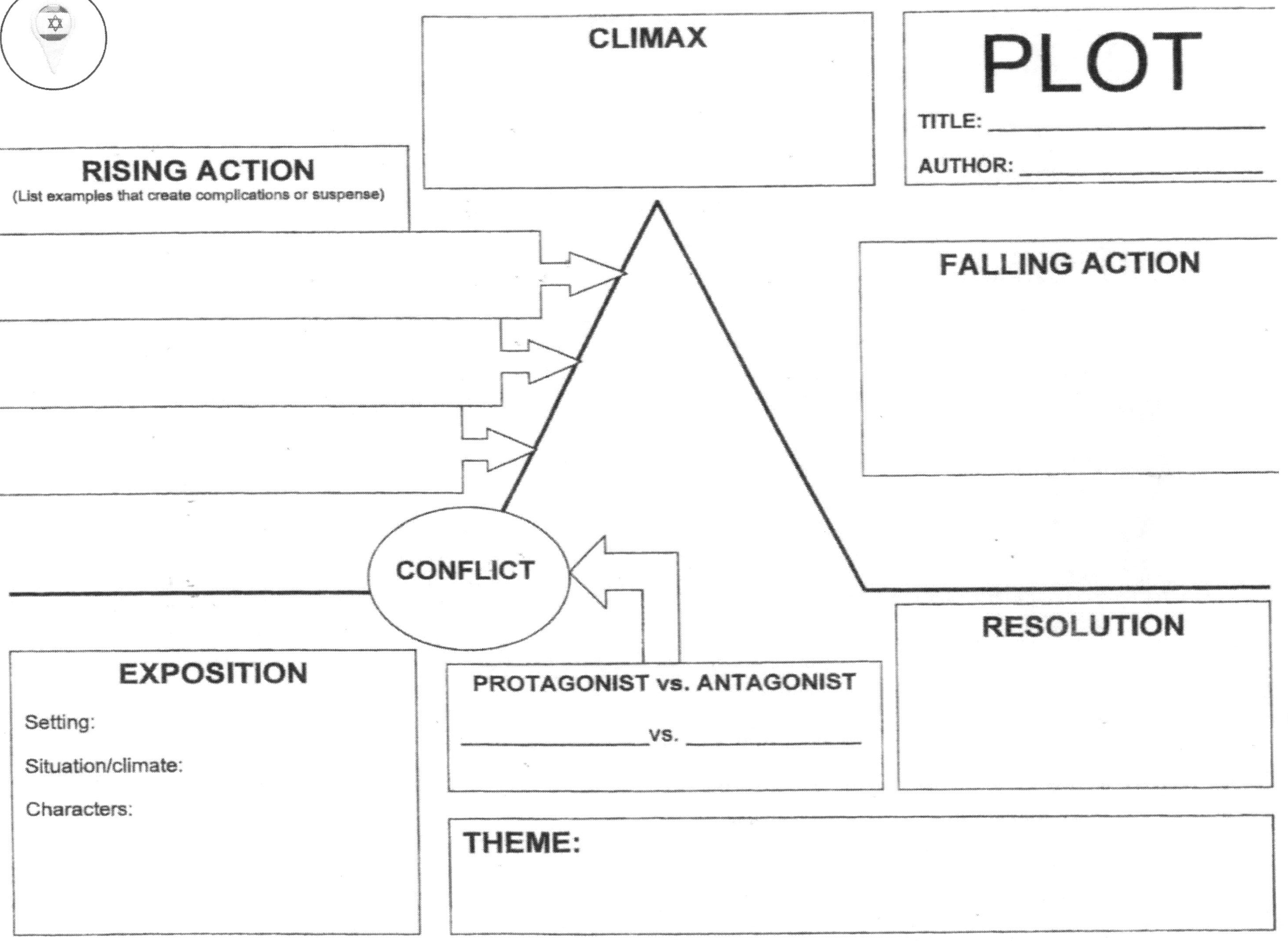
CLIMAX
PLOT
TITLE: ____
AUTHOR: ____
RISING ACTION
(List examples that create complications or suspense)
FALLING ACTION
CONFLICT
RESOLUTION
EXPOSITION
Setting:
Situation/climate:
Characters:
PROTAGONIST vs. ANTAGONIST
____ vs. ____
THEME:

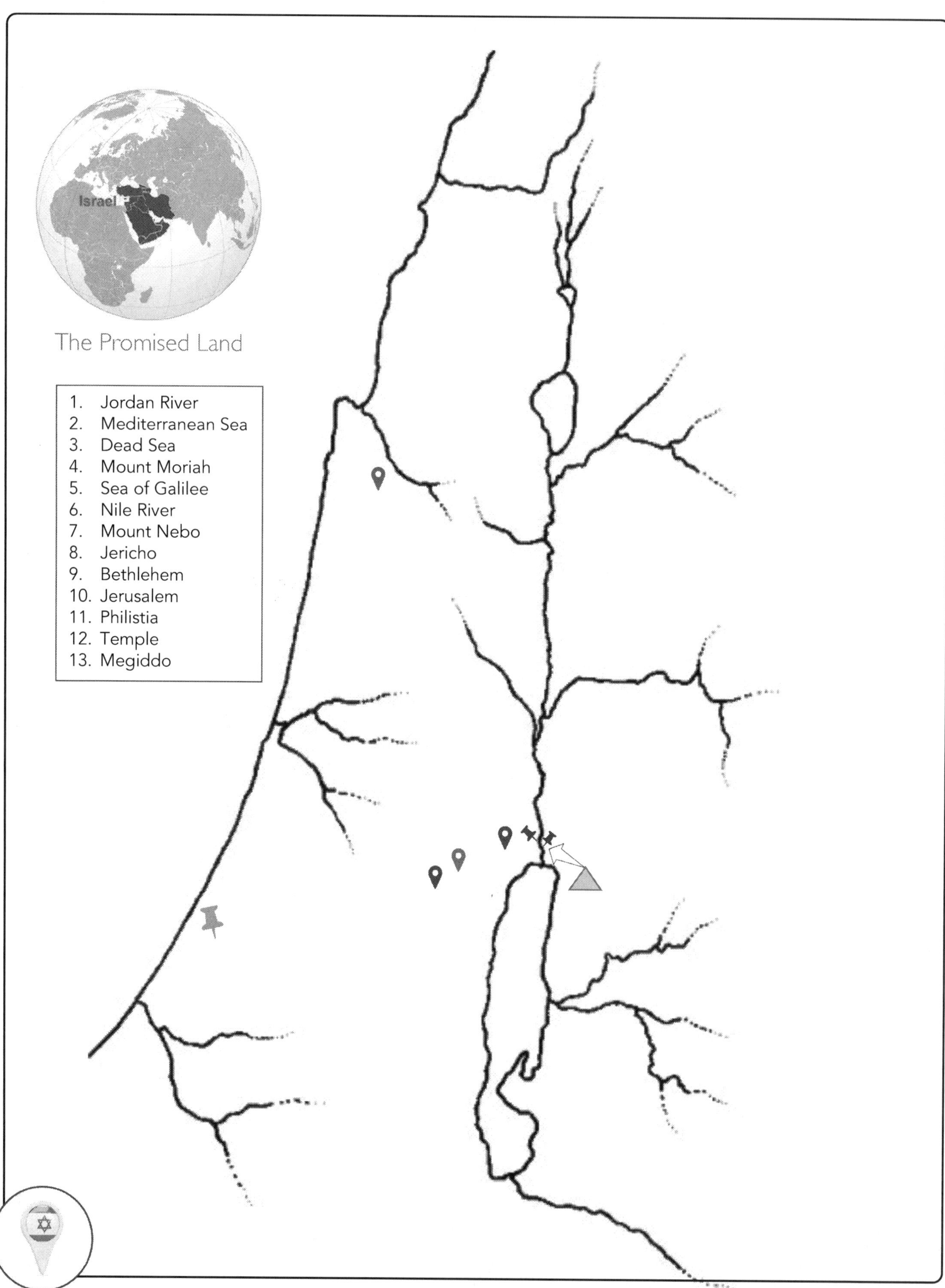
Israel
The Promised Land
1. Jordan River
2. Mediterranean Sea
3. Dead Sea
4. Mount Moriah
5. Sea of Galilee
6. Nile River
7. Mount Nebo
8. Jericho
9. Bethlehem
10. Jerusalem
11. Philistia
12. Temple
13. Megiddo

Character Study. Joshua; "Yahweh, God is Salvation"

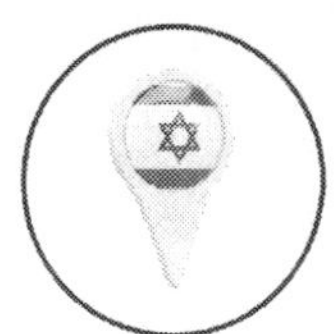

Examine the life of Joshua.
One of only two men to leave Egypt and enter The Promised Land

What were the beliefs and convictions of Joshua? How do you know?

What private thoughts from Joshua are revealed to us?

What are the actions or events from the life of Joshua that shaped him into the man he was and the one he would become?

How would you describe the character of Joshua (be sure to answer why and explain your response with references).

What does the life of Joshua teach me about faithfulness?

What does his life reveal to us about God?

What does his life reveal to me about myself?

Joshua… YWH, God is salvation

Promised Land

• Moses	Cusp of the land
• Joshua	Conquer the land
• Judges	Circles of sin in the land
• King Saul	No heart
• King David	Whole Heart
• King Solomon	Divided Heart
• Divided Kingdom	Israel, Judah
• Exile	Assyria, Babylon, Persia

Who was Joshua?

- Joshua means: YWH, God is salvation.
- Jesus' name in Hebrew is Joshua.
- Joshua crosses the Jordan river.
- Joshua conquers and settles the land.

Judges… The tragic cycle of sin

After that whole generation had been gathered to their ancestors, another generation grew up who knew neither the LORD nor what he had done for Israel.

Then the Israelites did evil in the eyes of the LORD and served the Baals.

They forsook the LORD, the God of their ancestors, who had brought them out of Egypt. They followed and worshiped various gods of the peoples around them. They aroused the LORD'S anger.

Judges 2:10-12

Whenever Israel went out to fight, the hand of the LORD was against them to defeat them, just as he had sworn to them. They were in great distress.

Then the LORD raised up judges, who saved them out of the hands of these raiders.

Judges 2:15-16

Whenever the Lord raised up a judge for them, he was with the judge and saved them out of the hands of their enemies as long as the judge lived; for the Lord relented because of their groaning under those who oppressed and afflicted them.

But when the judge died, the people returned to ways even more corrupt than those of their ancestors, following other gods and serving and worshiping them. They refused to give up their evil practices and stubborn ways.

Judges 2:18-19

In those days there was no king in Israel.
Everyone did what was right in his own eyes.

Judges 17:6

Character Study. Compare and Contrast the lives of Samuel & Saul

Examine the life of Samuel. The boy who was found in the presence of God

What were the beliefs and convictions of Samuel? How do you know?

What private thoughts from Samuel are revealed to us?

What are the actions or events from the life of Samuel that shaped him into the man he was and the one he would become?

How would you describe the character of Samuel (be sure to answer why and explain your response with references).

What does the life of Samuel teach me about faithfulness?

BELIEFS

What does his life reveal to us about God?

VALUES

ACTIONS

What does his life reveal to me about myself?

HABITS

Understanding the role of prophet, priest & king

Saul – No heart.
David – Whole heart.
Solomon – Divided heart.

Observations

Reflections

Character Study. Compare and Contrast the lives of Samuel & Saul

Examine the life of Saul. A king who would be found hiding among the donkeys and the baggage.

What were the beliefs and convictions of Saul? How do you know?

What private thoughts from Saul are revealed to us?

What are the actions or events from the life of Saul that shaped him into the man he was and the one he would become?

How would you describe the character of Saul (be sure to answer why and explain your response with references).

What does the life of Saul teach me about faithfulness?

BELIEFS

What does his life reveal to us about God?

VALUES

ACTIONS

What does his life reveal to me about myself?

HABITS

King David… The Shepherd who would become King

How did God use trials and giant in the life of David?

How does God use trials to invite me to trust Him?

Explain how God uses trials to transform us.

How do the Psalms invite me to approach God with authenticity?

Examine how David communicates with God in the Psalms and write a personal Psalm that reflect my current understanding and approach to God

Character Study. Examine the early life of David

Examine the shepherd boy who would kill a giant

What were the early beliefs and convictions of David? How do you know?

What private thoughts from David are revealed to us?

What are the actions or events from the life of David that shaped him into the man he was and the one he would become?

How would you describe the character of David (be sure to answer why and explain your response with references).

What does the early life of David teach me about faithfulness?

BELIEFS

What does his life reveal to us about God?

VALUES

What does his life reveal to me about myself?

ACTIONS

HABITS

King David... A man after God's own heart

1. Why does God choose to bring David into his redemptive story?

2. What are the elements of God's covenant with David?

3. David is referred to as a man after God's own heart? Why?

4. How do I become a man or woman after God's heart?

Character Study. Examine the Middle years of the life of King David

Examine the fugitive who would become the King.

What were the beliefs and convictions of David during his time as a fugitive and during his early years as the King of Israel? How do you know?

What private thoughts from David are revealed to us from this time?

What are the actions or events from the life of David from this time that shaped him into the man he was and the one he would become?

How would you describe the character of David during this time period of his life, (be sure to answer why and explain your response with references).

What does this season in the life of David teach me?

What does his life reveal to us about God?

What does his life reveal to me about myself?

King David... Failed Father & Fugitive

David, A life in review

Part I.

- An Important Visit, 1 Samuel 16:1-12
- The Spirit of the Lord, 1 Samuel 16:13; 17:34-37
- Playing for the King, 1 Samuel 16:14-17:11
- Goliath, 1 Samuel 17:12-18:16
- A King's Jealousy, 1 Samuel 18:17-20:42

Part II.

- On the Run, 1 Samuel 21:1-24:4
- A Chance at Revenge, 1 Samuel 24:1-27:8
- Becoming King, 1 Samuel 29:1-2 Samuel 5:25
- Jerusalem, 2 Samuel 5:6-10; 6:1-7, 29; 9: 1-9; 11:1-27

Part III.

- Sin, Repentance, and Punishment, 2 Samuel 12:1-23
- A Family in Tatters, 2 Samuel 13:1-17:23
- Descendants on the Throne, 2 Samuel 17:24-19:15; 21:15-17; 23:1-39; 1 Kings 1:5-2:12

Character Study. Examine the latter years of the life of King David

Examine the murderer who would become a fugitive.

What were the beliefs and convictions of David during this last phase of his life? What changed?

What private thoughts from David are revealed to us from this time?

What are the actions or events from the life of David from this time that shaped him into the man he was and the one he would become?

How would you describe the character of David during this time period of his life, (be sure to answer why and explain your response with references).

What does this season in the life of David teach me?

Beliefs

What does his life reveal to us about God?

Values

What does his life reveal to me about myself?

Actions

Habits

The altar of incense

"Make an altar of acacia wood for burning incense. 2 It is to be square, a cubit long and a cubit wide, and two cubits high its horns of one piece with it. 3 Overlay the top and all the sides and the horns with pure gold, and make a gold molding around it. 4 Make two gold rings for the altar below the molding—two on each of the opposite sides—to hold the poles used to carry it. 5 Make the poles of acacia wood and overlay them with gold. 6 Put the altar in front of the curtain that shields the ark of the covenant law—before the atonement cover that is over the tablets of the covenant law—where I will meet with you.
7 "Aaron must burn fragrant incense on the altar every morning when he tends the lamps. 8 He must burn incense again when he lights the lamps at twilight so incense will burn regularly before the Lord for the generations to come. 9 Do not offer on this altar any other incense or any burnt offering or grain offering, and do not pour a drink offering on it. 10 Once a year Aaron shall make atonement on its horns. This annual atonement must be made with the blood of the atoning sin offering for the generations to come. It is most holy to the Lord."

Exodus 30:1-2

The Oriental Museum Chicago, Illinois

What was found in Tel Megiddo?

Solomon made an alliance with Pharaoh king of Egypt and married his daughter. He brought her to the City of David until he finished building his palace and the temple of the Lord, and the wall around Jerusalem. The people, however, were still sacrificing at the high places, because a temple had not yet been built for the Name of the Lord. Solomon showed his love for the Lord by walking according to the instructions given him by his father David, ***except that he offered sacrifices and burned incense on the high places.***
The king went to Gibeon to offer sacrifices, for that was the most important high place, and Solomon offered a thousand burnt offerings on that altar. 5 At Gibeon the Lord appeared to Solomon during the night in a dream, and God said, "Ask for whatever you want me to give you."

1 Kings 3:1-5

Character Study. Examine the irony of the life of Solomon

Examine the life of Solomon. A wise king who would act like a fool.

What were the beliefs and convictions of Solomon? How do you know?

What private thoughts from Solomon are revealed to us?

What are the actions or events from the life of Solomon that shaped him into the man he was and the one he would become?

How would you describe the character of Solomon (be sure to answer why and explain your response with references).

What does the life of Solomon teach me about faithfulness?

What does his life reveal to us about God?

What does his life reveal to me about myself?

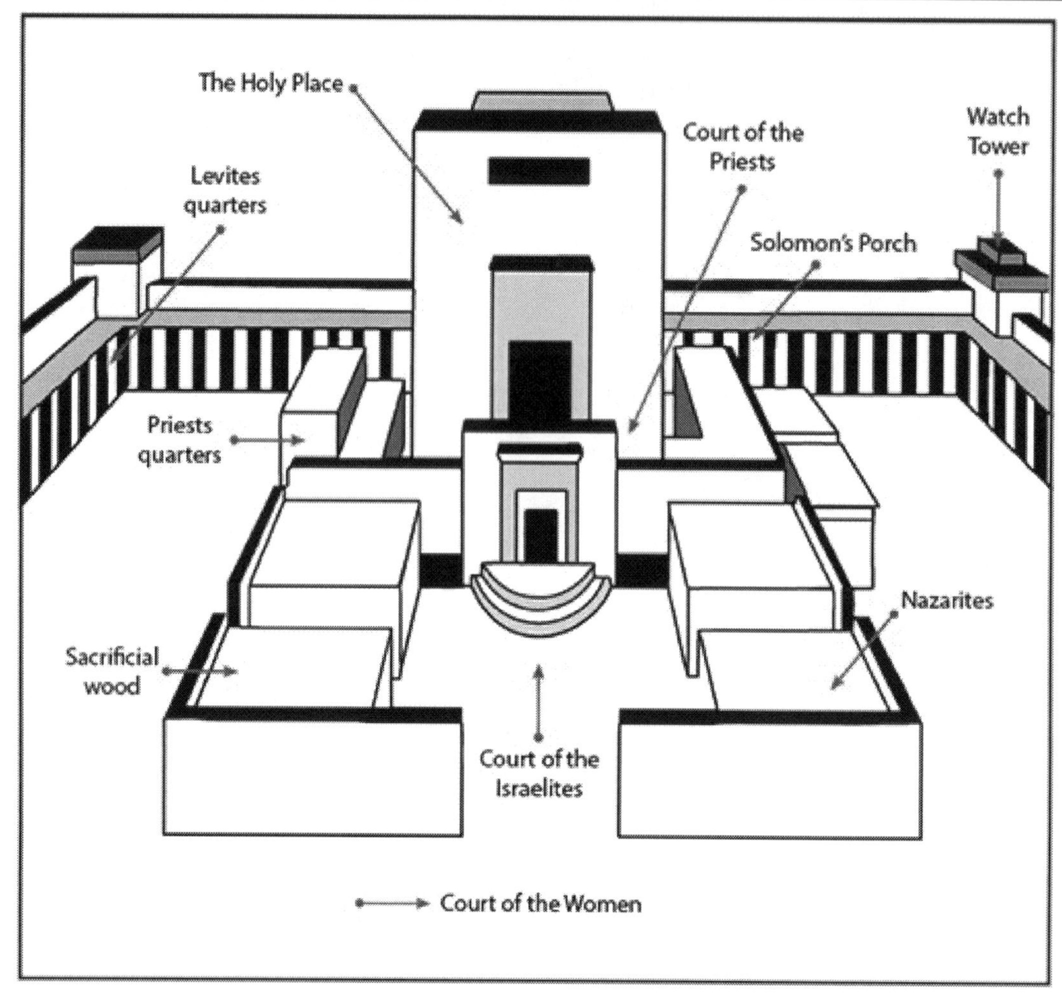

Temple. How is the temple the convergence of each of the threads?

Blue.	Scarlet.
Purple.	Gold.

HISTORY

THE MISSION OF GOD

AND THE SECRET OF THE GOLDEN THREAD

proximity

Can God be trusted?

Learning to love God's Word

"Holy, holy, holy is the LORD God Almighty; heaven and earth are full of his glory!'"

Isaiah 6:1–3

What is the learning goal for Proximity?

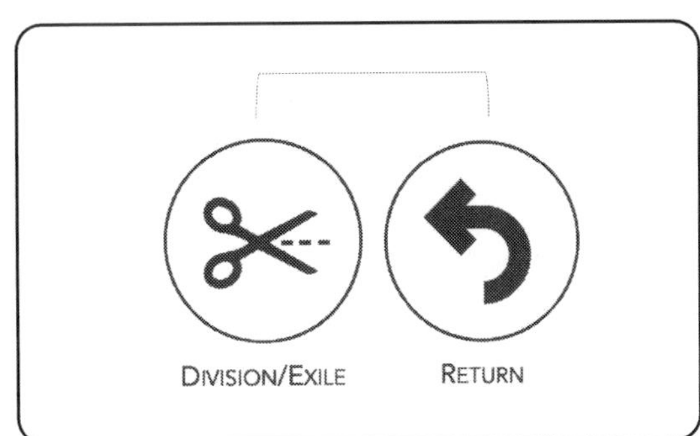

Proximity: nearness in space, time, or relationship.

One theme that has continued throughout the plot of the Hebrew Bible is the motif of physical proximity to the presence of God being reflective of spiritual proximity.

In the Garden of Eden, we learn that man and God shared space until the shame from their sin made Adam and Eve want to hide from the presence of God.

Throughout the plot, we have seen how God invites people into His presence. We have also seen how He creates opportunities for people to enjoy His presence. And we have seen how humanity has continually sought to remove themselves or forgotten to keep the habit of His presence.

We have seen this pattern in Eden, on Sinai, with the Tabernacle, and now we will see it again with The Temple of Solomon.

Do you remember how Israel was supposed to be a Kingdom of priests?

A nation that was uniquely set apart from the world as a special reflection of the glory of God.

But consider the actions and desires of the people. First, they desired to be like everyone else, so they begged God for a King. Second, the King they desired failed to lead them into the presence of God.

Then the second King, David, the man after God's own heart would lose focus, and his own heart would lead him into adultery, murder, and he would finish his life as an absentee father.

Finally, there was Solomon, a man conflicted. He was never sure if he loved God or if he was in love with his 1,000 foreign wives. Did you catch the keyword in the last sentence? Believe it or not, it wasn't the 1,000, as mind-boggling as that is, it was the word foreign.

Remember the purpose of the sons of Israel.
To be set apart. To be a royal priesthood that uniquely reflected the glory of God. But Solomon had a conflicted heart.

He desired wisdom, but his life and his lifestyle led his heart to be divided. Unfortunately, as went the heart of the King so followed the people of Israel.

Soon the nation was divided, and like Solomon, both the people of Israel grew further away from God both physically and spiritually.

Proximity; Division & Failure

Setting:
Where:

When:

Major Characters:

Minor Characters:

Plot/Problem:

Event 1:

Event 2:

Event 3:

Outcome:

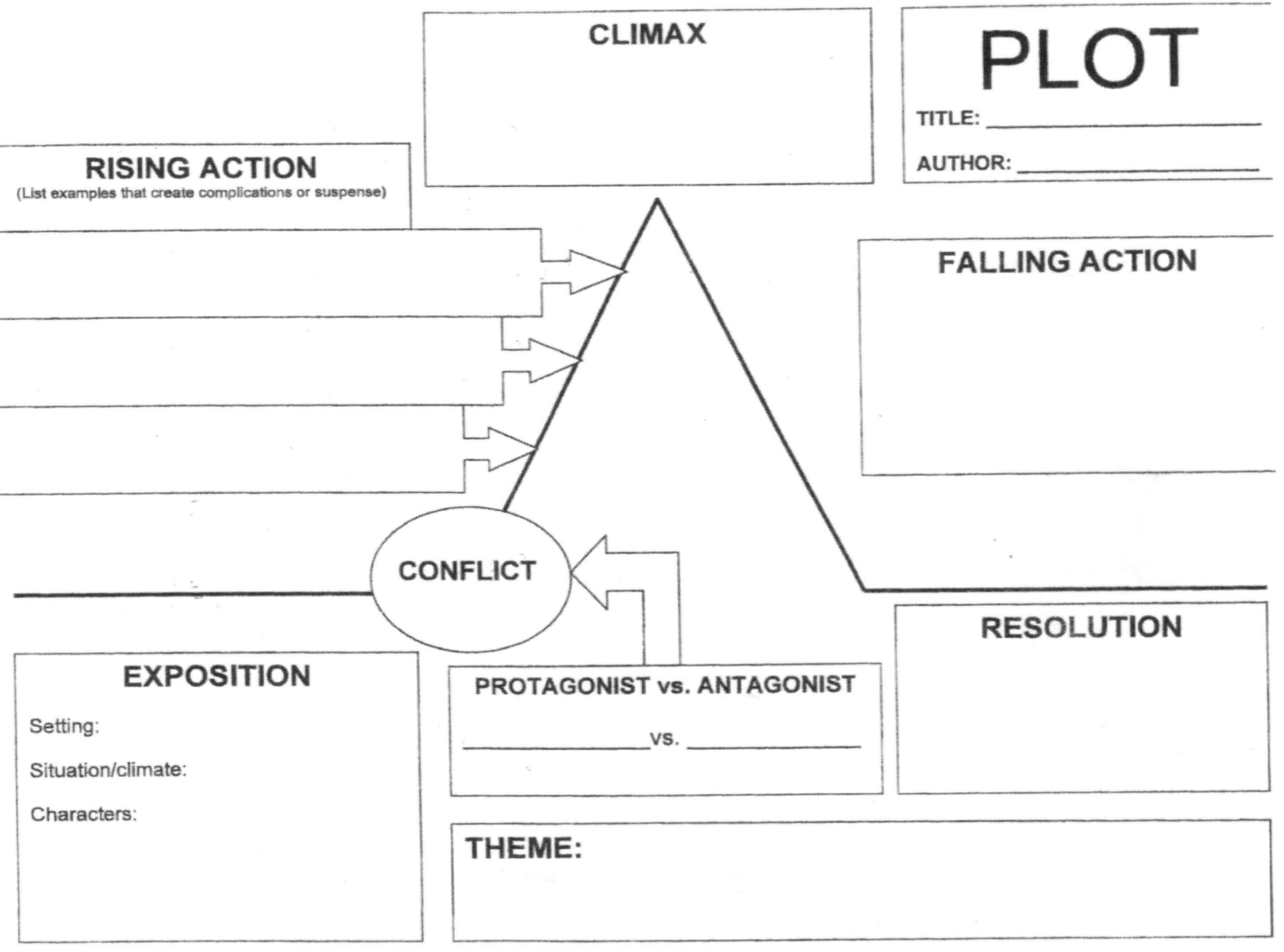
CLIMAX
PLOT
TITLE:
AUTHOR:
RISING ACTION
(List examples that create complications or suspense)
FALLING ACTION
CONFLICT
RESOLUTION
EXPOSITION
Setting:
Situation/climate:
Characters:
PROTAGONIST vs. ANTAGONIST
vs.
THEME:

Explain and Illustrate

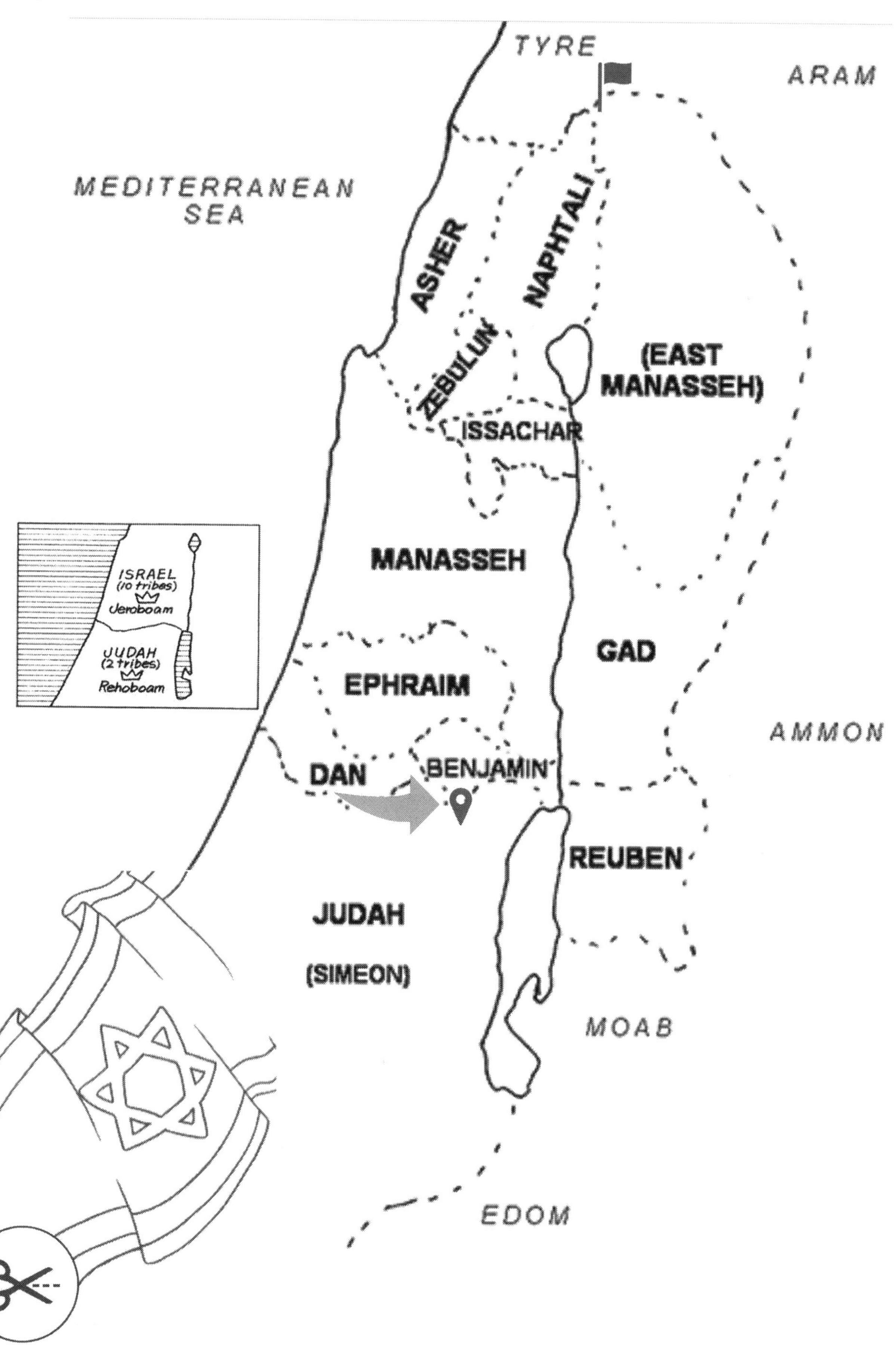

What happens in the text?

Division – Israel, Judah

- Solomon's divided heart leads to a divided Kingdom.
- His son follows foolish advice.
- His former advisor rebels.
- The Kingdom is divided.
- His son, Rehoboam, is left with the southern two
- tribes called Judah.
- His former advisor, Jeroboam, takes the 10 northern tribes and calls them Israel.
- Israel – 10 tribes in the North
- Judah – 2 tribes in the South
- Both Israel and Judah rebel against God leading to the periods of exile.

Exile – Return

- Assyria invades Israel – lost tribes.
- Babylon invades Judah – lost temple.
- Persia conquers Babylon, - Jews return.

What might it look like in my life?

- Why do I sometimes forget the Lord and what he has done for me and other times remember the gospel?
- When I see with spiritual eyes the work of God in my life and others, I reflect his image by rejoicing in his grace and celebrating his goodness.
- When I do not see how God is working due to spiritual blindness because of idols in my heart, I fail to worship God and grow in the knowledge of the Lord.
- Why do I sometimes feel that God is clearly leading me and other times I feel like I need to lead the way?
- When I see God's meaning in his Word and understand his purposes, I reflect his image by repenting of sin and trusting his way so that he may glorify himself through me.
- When I neglect to seek understanding of God's Word or neglect his Word all-together, I do not know how to reflect his image and so seek my own way which comes from a selfish heart controlled by idolatry like the people of Israel and Judah did.

What things distract me from the glory of God and true worship?
What are idols that can take my hearts?

Beliefs

Values

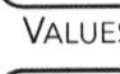

Actions

Habits

How do I build a foundation that lasts?

Proverbs 9:10 states that; "Fear of the Lord is the foundation of wisdom. Knowledge of the Holy One results in good judgement."

Fast forward several hundred years to the time of Christ. Students studying the Hebrew Scriptures at the time of Christ would have received these words as much more than just good advice or a cute proverb.

They believed that the future of their nation depended on the decisions that they made and how they approached God.

The Jewish people during the time of Jesus were living in the land of Israel under Roman occupation and their greatest longing was for God to send a Messiah to raise an army to remove the Romans.

If you would have asked the average Jewish student what they **trusted**, what they **feared** and where they placed their **hope**, then you would have probably have heard that:

- **They Trusted** the promises of the God of Abraham, Isaac and Jacob as revealed in the Tanakh (the name for the Hebrew Scriptures).
- **They Feared** disobedience to the laws of God would result in greater abuse from the Roman soldiers who occupied their land.
- **They Hoped** that they obeyed God's laws that He would send a Messiah to deliver His people from the Romans and allow them to experience the full blessings of God.

How do I approach God?

The reason for these responses was because the first five books of the **Tanakh**, known as the **Torah**, taught that if the people of God obeyed His laws with all of their hearts that He would bless them and remove their enemies.

The Torah also taught that if the people failed to obey God's laws or if they worshipped other gods that they would experience God's judgement and their enemies would rule over them.

These are the promises that God kept during the time after the life of King Solomon.

The disobedience of the people of Israel and the proximity of their hearts results in their disobedience to His covenant. The result, was the God kept His promise and the people experienced the consequences of their actions.

"These are the commands, decrees and laws the Lord your God directed me to teach you to observe in the land that you are crossing the Jordan to possess, 2 so that you, your children and their children after them may fear the Lord your God as long as you live by keeping all his decrees and commands that I give you, and so that you may enjoy long life. 3 Hear, Israel, and be careful to obey so that it may go well with you and that you may increase greatly in a land flowing with milk and honey, just as the Lord, the God of your ancestors, promised you.

4 Hear, O Israel: The Lord our God, the Lord is one. 5 Love the Lord your God with all your heart and with all your soul and with all your strength. 6 These commandments that I give you today are to be on your hearts. 7 Impress them on your children. Talk about them when you sit at home and when you walk along the road, when you lie down and when you get up. 8 Tie them as symbols on your hands and bind them on your foreheads. 9 Write them on the doorframes of your houses and on your gates.

Deuteronomy 6:1-10

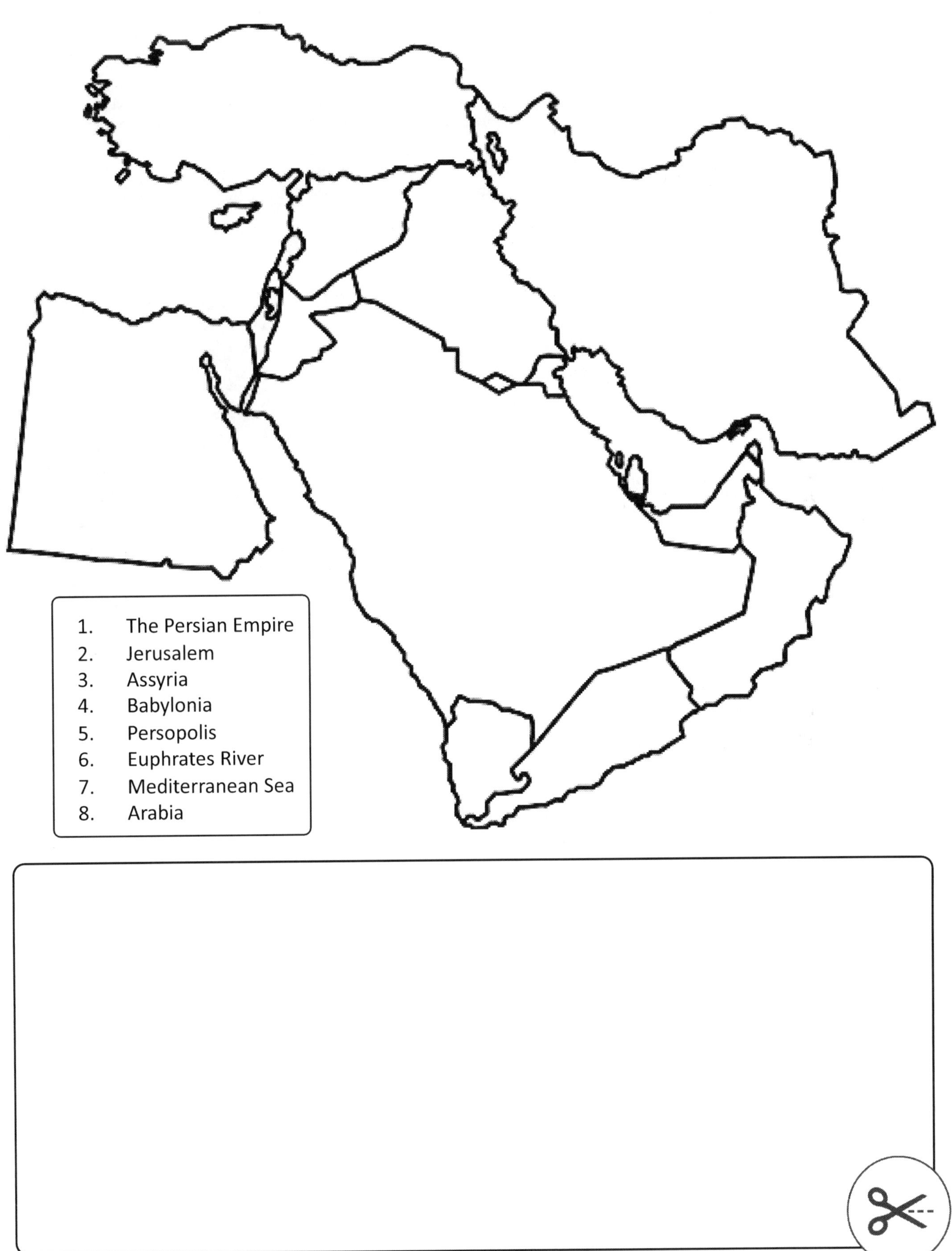
1. The Persian Empire
2. Jerusalem
3. Assyria
4. Babylonia
5. Persopolis
6. Euphrates River
7. Mediterranean Sea
8. Arabia

Assyria was known for being ruthless and for their terrifying treatment of those they conquered. They were both hated and feared by the countries they went to battle against. They had large armies that were equipped with the latest military innovations that were designed to cause pain and large amounts of damage.

The capital city, Nineveh, was known for idolatry, child sacrifice and perverse sexual activity (2 Kings 17:16-18). Today the modern city of Nineveh is Mosul, located in northern Iraq on the eastern bank of the Tigris river.

This is the city that Yahweh, instructed Jonah to go and preach the message of repentance and the city where Jonah refused. In the mind of Jonah, the people of this city were beyond saving, but in the mind of God, His desire was (and still is) for the entire world to reflect His glory.

Because of their sin, the 10 northern tribes of Israel were brutally destroyed by the Assyrians. The promised judgement of God from Deuteronomy was kept and the 10 tribes ceased existence. The remnant who remained would be forced to marry people of other ethnic groups and religions. By the time that Jesus walked in Israel, these people would be known as the Samaritans.

However, there is a second act to the story of the Assyrians and the two remaining tribes of Judah in the southern part of the land of Israel.

Statue of "*the big fish*" a few blocks from The Mediterranean Sea in historic Joffa, Israel (Tel Aviv).

Pause and Reflect. In light of this information, does it change or impact your thoughts about Jonah and his desire to obey God by going to Nineveh? Why or why not?

ASSYRIA CONQUERS THE 10 NORTHERN TRIBES

Hezekiah, one of the few kings who actually led the people to humble themselves before God and brought out repentance and reform among the people in the remaining two tribes.

Around 700 BC, the new King of Assyria, a man of war with a reputation for viciousness and complete destruction of those he conquered set his sites on the remaining Israelites.

His invasion of Judah was preceded by the complete destruction of several cities. Sennacherib's own historical accounts claim that he destroyed 46 walled cities and deported over 200,000 captives. These historical accounts are written on clay cylinders that are known as prisms and are available to be viewed in museums in Chicago, London and Paris.

Archeologists have discovered a palace that was built by Assyrian captives, including Israelites. This massive palace had over 70 halls and chambers and was called, The Palace without a Rival."

Inside of it there were statues of winged bulls and large stone panels that commemorated the destruction of the cities of Judah, including the siege of Lachish. These panels are available in The Oriental Museum in Chicago, The British Museum in London and The Louvre in Paris. Other impressively large artifacts known as lamassu and weighing over 33 tons are available to be seen in these same museums.

The panels depicting the battles are also impressive. With over 9,843 ft of incredibly graphic illustrations of people who being flayed alive, while other images show people having their tongues removed. The pictures, which would have been the equivalent of today's selfie, show long lines of prisoners being led away with piles of heads without bodies surrounding the king.

Each of the stone carvings are specific with the images of the army celebrating victories and showing off the spoils of war. One image contains the words, of Babylon, "It's inhabitants, young and old, I did not spare, and with their corpses I filled the streets of the city."

Other panels graphically display Israelite prisoners being impaled on stakes outside of the city walls.

What is amazing is that a reading of Sennacherib's journal (the prism) reads exactly like the Bible. When placed side by side the historic accounts from Sennacherib's reflection and the historic account recorded in the Bible are the same story.

At one point, Sennacherib even brags that he has laid siege to the city of Jerusalem and has made King Hezekiah a prisoner, "like a bird in a cage."

However, that is oddly where Sennacherib's account of the battle ends.

Unlike every other battle where Sennacherib tells of the conquest and the beheadings and the number of captives brought back to Assyria, the story of the siege of Jerusalem stops with the illustration of Hezekiah trapped like a bird in a cage.

If we only had Sennacherib's account then we would be left thinking that something didn't add up. Wouldn't the capture of Jerusalem be the crowning achievement of his conquests? Wouldn't Sennacherib go out of his way to tell of the destruction of Jerusalem and the fate of King Hezekiah of the Jews? Wouldn't there be panels that illustrate the story of the conquest, capture and captives?

The answer is yes. If Sennacherib and his army would have defeated Jerusalem and killed King Hezekiah then most certainly all of those things would be true and we would be able to read the non-biblical historical record.

But those things were not recorded by Sennacherib because that is not what happened next.

Certainly the Biblical account and the account available through Sennacherib's personal records match identically, even to the point of the siege and the probable defeat and destruction of Jerusalem, but where Sennacherib saves embarrassment by ending the story before it is fully completed, the Bible records what happens next.

The Biblical record of what happened next informs us that The Angel of The Lord went into the Assyrian camp in the middle of the night and killed 185,000 soldiers. The result was that Sennacherib had no choice but to retreat in defeat. His vast army had been wiped out by the God of King Hezekiah (Isaiah 37:14-21,36).

Hezekiah had prepared the people for a military battle but ultimately he had led them through the process of repentance and his trust was in in God, not himself or his army.

ASSYRIA CONQUERS
THE 10 NORTHERN TRIBES

BABYLON CONQUERS
THE 2 SOUTHERN TRIBES

The second exile involved the remaining 2 Southern Tribes of Judah and included the loss of Jerusalem and Temple.

"At that time the officers of Nebuchadnezzar king of Babylon advanced on Jerusalem and laid siege to it," 2 Kings 24:10

"So in the ninth year of Zedekiah's reign, on the tenth day of the tenth month, Nebuchadnezzar king of Babylon marched against Jerusalem with his whole army. He encamped outside the city and built siege works all around it."

2 Kings 25:1

"Nebuchadnezzar also took to Babylon articles from the temple of the Lord and put them in his temple there. He carried to Babylon all the articles from the temple of God, both large and small, and the treasures of the Lord's temple and the treasures of the king and his officials."

2 Chronicles 36:7, 18

Tiles from the Processional Way leading to The Ishtar Gate of ancient Babylon displayed at the Chicago Oriental Museum
http://www.atour.com/education/20110605a.html

How does archeology help us build trust in the Bible?

Shadrach, Meshach and Abednego

Then Nebuchadnezzar was furious with Shadrach, Meshach and Abednego, and his attitude toward them changed. He ordered the furnace heated seven times hotter than usual and commanded some of the strongest soldiers in his army to tie up Shadrach, Meshach and Abednego and throw them into the blazing furnace. So these men, wearing their robes, trousers, turbans and other clothes, were bound and thrown into the blazing furnace. The king's command was so urgent and the furnace so hot that the flames of the fire killed the soldiers who took up Shadrach, Meshach and Abednego, and these three men, firmly tied, fell into the blazing furnace.

Daniel 3:19-23

PERSIA CONQUERS BABYLON

Persia. The largest of the empires. God uses the Persian King Cyrus to allow the Jews to return to Jerusalem and rebuild the temple.

How does archeology help us build trust in the Bible?

The story of Esther.

On the third day Esther put on her royal robes and stood in the inner court of the palace, in front of the king's hall. The king was sitting on his royal throne in the hall, facing the entrance.

Esther 5:1

What do the lives of the young men and women living in exile in Assyria, Babylon and Persia who chose to follow and honor God with their lives teach me about proximity?

http://classconnection.s3.amazonaws.com/1875/flashcards/714308/jpg/palace-of-darius-i-and-xerxes3.jpg

The Purim Spiel

Spiel is a Yiddish word meaning a "play" or "skit." A Purim spiel is actually a dramatic presentation of the events outlined in the Book of Esther. Featuring the main characters, such as King Ahasuerus, Mordecai, Esther, and the wicked Haman, the Purim spiel was a folk-inspired custom providing an opportunity for crowds to cheer the heroes (Mordecai and Esther) and boo the villains (Haman).

Introduction

Reader 1: Intrigue. Romance. Action. Betrayal. Loyalty. Royalty. Villains. Heroes.
This is the story of Purim.

Reader 2: Hello and welcome to our Purim Spiel. You are about to hear the story of Purim, a holiday which celebrates the salvation of the Jewish people from the wicked Haman. Purim is one of the most joyous holidays because it is a time when Jews dress up, listen to the entertaining tale of Purim, eat delicious food, celebrate numerous traditions, and celebrate with family and friends.

Reader 1: Purim takes place on the 14th day of Adar, which is in the 12th month of the Jewish calendar. On this holiday, everyone dresses up in costumes and goes to synagogue to hear the reading of this tale. The biblical story of Purim is found in the "Megillah," also known as the book of Esther.

During this public reading, whenever the name "Haman" is said in the story, everyone "boos," stomps their feet, and rings their groggers, otherwise known as noisemakers, to block out the evil Haman's name.

Reader 2: This means that we are going to need your help. Every time you hear the name "Haman" in the story, make as much noise as possible with your hands, feet, and groggers in order to block out his name.
So please sit back, relax, and get your groggers ready, as we present the story of Purim.

Scene 1

Narrator: Long ago, in the 6th century BCE, there lived a king named Achashverosh. In the 3rd year of his reign of the Persian Empire, in the city of Shushan, King Achashverosh decided to throw an extravagant party.

Enter King Achashverosh, Queen Vashti, and the partygoers.
They talk and laugh; King A drinks a lot

King A: Wife, I have a favor to ask of you. **Vashti:** What is it dear?

King A: Well, this is a great party and all... Vashti: (*distractedly)* Yes, honey?

King A: But I know what would make it even better!

Vashti: (*slightly exasperated)* What?

King A: Could you...dance in front of my guests, please? You know… Zumba®. *(King laughs at his idea)*

Vashti: Wait, what?

King A: I just think that would really get this party started!

Vashti: No way. Uh-uh. Not a chance!

King A: *(Drawing himself taller)* I said, I, the king of this land, would like you to dance and lead everyone in some of that fun party dancing.. Now!

The party has gone silent and people stare at the drama unfolding.

Vashti: (*Bossily)* And I, as the queen, say that it's not going to happen!

A stare-off. The king and queen look at each other to see who will break first.

Vashti: Not. A. Chance!

King A: (*Beat. A moment of confusion for the king. Then...)* Fine. You refuse to do what your king asks, and in front of my subjects as well. You must be punished!

Vashti: (*disbelieving) Seriously? I've seen these people try to dance, they have no groove. I would be totally wasting my time and talent.*

King A: Take her away! The King decreases this: off with her head!

Vashti: No! Wait!
Two security guys in suits come and grasp Vashti, one on each arm.

Vashti: (*gasps theatrically)* Nooo!

Vashti is dragged offstage. Scene.

Scene 2

The three contestants are sitting on stool and the King is standing on the other side of the stage, the MC(can be another character)is standing in between them.

Narrator: The king then went on a search to find a new queen by having a beauty pageant.

Beauty Pageant MC: The King is looking for a new bride! Will it be Contestant 1, 2, or 3? Let's find out! Now before we start why don't we have each girl tell us something about herself! (goes to contestant number 1, Let's start with you.

Contestant #1: I'm Naarah, I love cotton candy and taking long walks on the beach!

MC: Fantastic! And how about contestant number 2?

Contestant #2: I'm Cabul, I enjoy working on my fighting skills.

MC: Fascinating! And Contestant number 3?

Contestant #3(Esther): I'm Esther, I like spending time with my family.

MC: Great, just great! Now in our first round we will ask our lovely contestants a question about themselves! Let's get started! The question is: If you could have one wish, what would it be? Contestant number 1?

Contestant # 1: I would wish for fame and fortune. *King makes a face.*

MC: Contestant number 2?

Contestant #2: I would wish for power. *King makes another face.*

MC: okay... Contestant 3?

Esther: Oh, I don't know. I guess I would wish for my friends and family to be safe and happy.
King looks pleased.

MC: Now, Your highness, which girl do you like best?

King carefully considers each girl. Girls try to look their best. King finishes with Esther.

King: This is the girl who shall be my bride.
Esther smiles uneasily. Other girls exit the stage in disappointment.

MC: And that ends today's exciting pageant.

Narrator: The King and Esther were soon married. The King was satisfied with his beautiful new bride, but he didn't know that his wife had a secret.

Esther (in soliloquy): I love the King, but I can't bring myself to tell him that I'm Jewish. If he discovers I have been concealing such an important matter, I am sure he will get rid of me. It is better for me to just hide the truth.

Scene 3

Narrator: Soon after this, Haman, the evil villain, became the new chief advisor of the King.

Haman: Now that I am chief advisor to the king, everyone must bow down to me! Haman: Bow down to me, peasants!
Mordecai walks by but doesn't bow.

Haman: Hey! You there! Why didn't you bow down to me?

Mordecai: I only bow down to God.
Mordecai walks away

Haman: (*to another peasant)* Peasant! Who was that man and why did he not bow down to me?? As the advisor to the king, I demand an answer!

Peasant: He is a Jew named Mordecai, sir. The Jews have a rule that they cannot bow down to anyone but God.

Haman: Thank you peasant, you shall be rewarded! You are dismissed. (*peasant leaves)*

Haman: I must destroy this Mordecai, and all the Jews with him...I shall create giant gallows to wipe out the disgusting Jewish population! I must go talk to the king... (*the king walks onto the stage)*

Haman: Oh, there you are, sir!

King A: Oh, hello Haman. I was just wandering around, admiring my country.

Haman: Good for you, sir......sir, I have discovered that there is a disgusting group of people here in Persia! They are called the Jewish people, but they call themselves "the chosen ones of God"! They don't keep our laws, such as bowing down to me, your chief advisor, they don't eat the same foods as we do, and they always celebrate holidays! If you give me your permission, I can destroy them for you!

King A: Yes, yes, whatever you would like...I'm going to go see what Esther is up to...
(*Achashverosh walks away*)

Haman: Success! (*Haman walks away the other way)*

Scene 4

Narrator: Mordechai, Esther's uncle, found out about Haman's evil plot to kill the Jews, and rushed to tell Esther. He told Esther that she had to take the fate of the Jews into her own hands. In order to do so, she needed to talk with the King. This was a very risky move of Esther's part, however, because it was forbidden to see the King without first being summoned. Therefore, Esther called for a three-day fast among the Jews in the city, to bring her luck.

Scene 5

Narrator: Esther then went to see the King to inform him that Haman was trying to kill her and all of her people.

Esther: My King, I have a request.

King: Anything you ask for will be granted, my Queen!

Esther: I wish that Haman and you attend a royal banquet tonight

King: Gladly

Scene 6

At the banquet, people stand around laughing with cups in hand and can chat quietly.

Narrator: At the banquet Achashverosh and Haman enjoyed themselves, but the King still wondered why Esther arranged the banquet in the first place.

King: Esther, again, what is your wish?

Esther: Only that you and Haman attend another banquet tomorrow night.

King: As you wish, my queen.

Haman: *(to Esther and King)* This has been a wonderful feast! I think I will walk some of these pounds off. Goodnight my King and your majesty.
Haman walks to other side of stage where Mordechai is standing.

Haman: *(In an angry tone)* Oh it's you...Jew. How dare you not bow to me! I will see you hanged for your lack of respect to me.
Haman storms off, as Mordechai stands his ground.

Haman: I will build a gallows for him and he will be hanged right away!

Next Scene. *Inside the King's chamber*

King: I cannot sleep! I feel as if I have forgotten something! Servant! what ever happened to that Jew who saved my life?

Servant: Nothing sir, he went about his way and was given no reward.

King: Send for Haman!

Haman: (Quietly before he sees the king) Now is my chance to ask for permission to hang that filthy Jew, Mordechai.

King: What should I do for the man that I want to honor?

Haman: He should be led around the city in royal attire upon a horse!

King: What a splendid idea!

Haman: I am so glad that you want to do this for *me*!

King: No No No I want to honor Mordechai.

Haman: Oh, I see. Good night, sir.
Haman confused leaves the room

Scene 7

Narrator: The next day, Ester and the King arrive at the second banquet.

King: Esther this is a fine banquet! Again, what is your wish!

Esther: My King, please spare my life and the life of my people!

King: What are you talking about!?

Esther: I am Jewish and I beg you to stop this massacre from taking place. Haman has ordered that all the Jews be killed, and that my uncle Mordechai will be killed on the gallows that Haman built himself!

King: What sort of treachery is this? HAMAN!!!!

Haman: *(Throwing himself before the king and queen)* Forgive me?!!!

King: How dare you!!! You will be hung by the very gallows that you built!

Narrator: Haman was killed along with his ten sons so his blood line would be erased.

Next Scene

Esther: Thank you my king!

King: I said I would grant you any wish my queen.

Mordechai : And because of your bravery and love for your people you have saved us Esther, and many thanks to you my King.

Traditions

Reader 3: After hearing these Purim tales, you may be wondering, what does one actually do to celebrate this holiday? Well, there are many traditions that make Purim so joyous and special. Part of the Purim festivities include eating "hamantaschen," which is a delicious pastry, recognizable for its three-cornered shape.

The name Hamantashen is known as a reference to Haman, the villain of the story. Hamantashen are made with many different fillings, including apple, cherry, chocolate, prunes, nuts, and poppy seed. These triangular cookies are said to either resemble Haman's three- cornered hat or his pointy ears. In Israel, these cookies are called "Oznei Haman," which is Hebrew for "Haman's ears."

Reader 4: Another custom that many follow is fasting the day before Purim. This is done in order to commemorate Esther's three-day fast that preceded the salvation of the Jews. After fasting, however, one of the requirements in the Book of Esther is to celebrate the occasion by eating a huge feast.

Reader 5: In addition, many people, especially children, enjoy dressing up on Purim. Costumes and masks are worn to disguise the wearer's identities, because mistaken identity plays a vital role in the story of Purim.

Reader 6: We hope that you have enjoyed this assembly and enjoy some Hamentaschen as well! Please return your groggers to the box on your way out of the auditorium. Thank you and you are all dismissed.

Esther's Hamentashen

Ingredients

- 4 eggs
- 1 cup of oil
- 1 ¼ cups of sugar
- 2 teaspoons of vanilla essence
- 3 teaspoons of baking powder
- 5 1/2 cups of flour
- Apricot, cherry, plum, or strawberry preserves

Directions

1. Preheat oven to 350 degrees.
2. Mix eggs, oil, sugar and vanilla.
3. Add baking powder and flour, and then knead until smooth.
4. Roll out very thin (1/8 inch) on a floured board, and then cut out circles with a drinking glass.
5. Place a spoonful of filling in the center of each circle.
6. Fold in three sides over the filling to form a triangle – making sure that the filling is visible in the center.
7. Bake at 350 for 15 minutes on a greased cookie sheet.

Adapted from: https://www.cjebaltimore.org/sites/default/files/Purim%20Assembly%20with%20Skit.pdf

HISTORY

THE MISSION OF GOD

AND THE SECRET OF THE GOLDEN THREAD

pause

Can God be trusted?

Learning to love God's Word

After this I looked, and there before me was a great multitude that no one could count, from every nation, tribe, people and language, standing before the throne and before the Lamb...All the angels were standing around the throne... They fell down on their faces before the throne and worshiped God,

Revelation 7:9-11

The Purple Thread

Scrambled word	Box numbers
DENE	20 219 259 227
RAK	25 158
BALBE	153 200 130 48
NIOGH PGSIRN	169 137 6 76 277 / 122 128 104 272 83
SEGRIT RERVI	99 238 218 175 136 / 222 235 16 265 197
SURTEAHEP VRREI	125 112 251 118 116 278 138 / 236 276 26 247
RAGGIZUT	284 146 258 162 43
RU	93 64
NACNAA	39 4 171 87
PYTGE	7 100 129
DARJON RIRVE	262 40 178 57 11 134 / 155 110 49 70 188
AESIRL	18 142 82 107 208
DIERMTEANANER SAE	77 151 15 225 51 91 260 165 123 209 285 / 149 1
MEASURLEJ	154 157 29 205 63 152
DEDA ASE	85 180 67 / 46 156
NOTMU HIAROM	199 62 177 73 68 / 210 13 72 212 59
JUADE	190 160 42 143
ASE FO GELLIEA	147 196 / 17 102 / 275 263 60 185
INLE RRIEV	28 189 207 / 141 239 217 131
ERD EAS	256 255 161 / 172 253 47

The Purple Thread

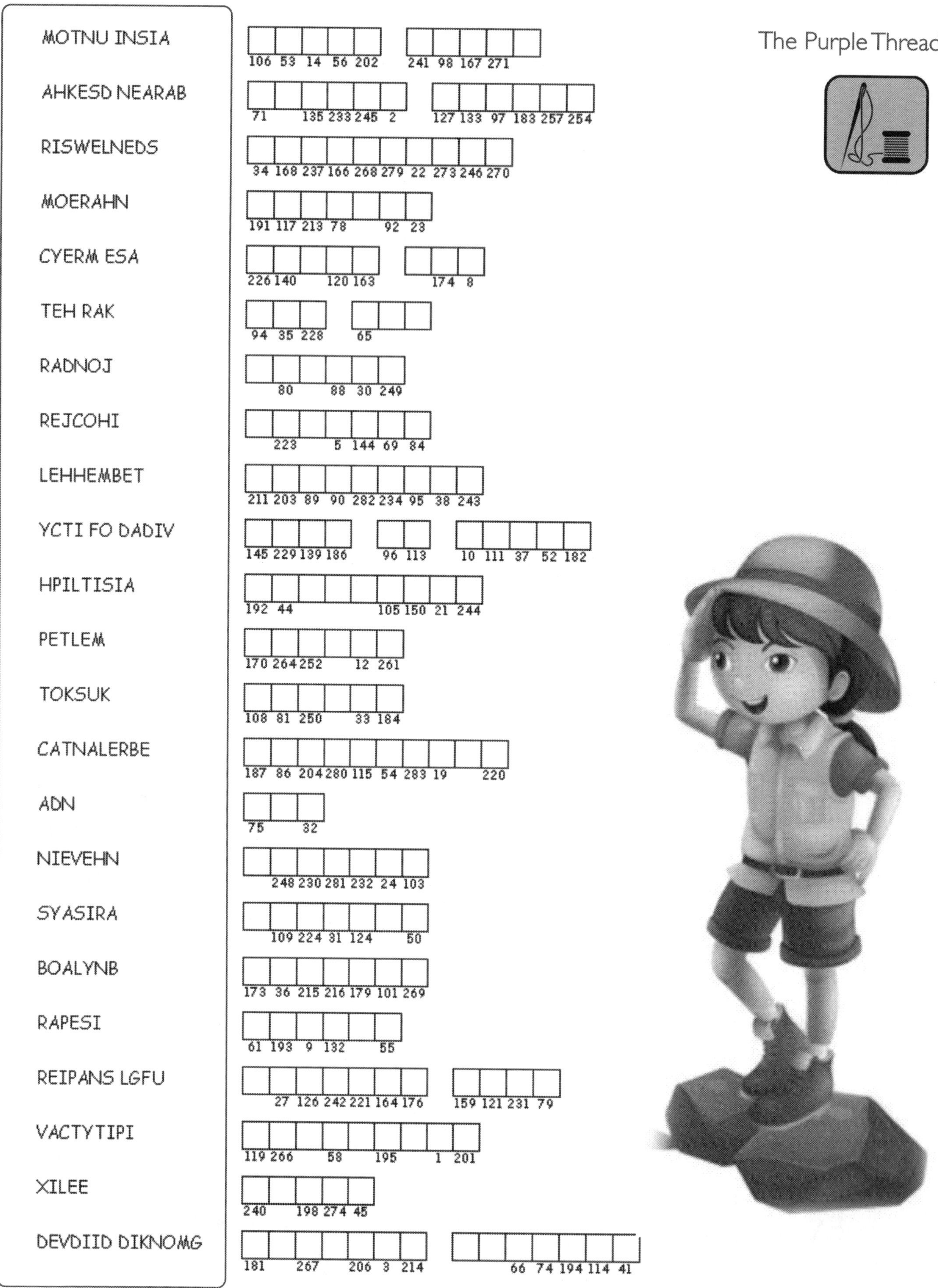

Scrambled Word	Number Clues
MOTNU INSIA	106 53 14 56 202 / 241 98 167 271
AHKESD NEARAB	71 135 233 245 2 / 127 133 97 183 257 254
RISWELNEDS	34 168 237 166 268 279 22 273 246 270
MOERAHN	191 117 213 78 92 23
CYERM ESA	226 140 120 163 / 174 8
TEH RAK	94 35 228 / 65
RADNOJ	80 88 30 249
REJCOHI	223 5 144 69 84
LEHHEMBET	211 203 89 90 282 234 95 38 243
YCTI FO DADIV	145 229 139 186 / 96 113 / 10 111 37 52 182
HPILTISIA	192 44 105 150 21 244
PETLEM	170 264 252 12 261
TOKSUK	108 81 250 33 184
CATNALERBE	187 86 204 280 115 54 283 19 220
ADN	75 32
NIEVEHN	248 230 281 232 24 103
SYASIRA	109 224 31 124 50
BOALYNB	173 36 215 216 179 101 269
RAPESI	61 193 9 132 55
REIPANS LGFU	27 126 242 221 164 176 / 159 121 231 79
VACTYTIPI	119 266 58 195 1 201
XILEE	240 198 274 45
DEVDIID DIKNOMG	181 267 206 3 214 / 66 74 194 114 41

The Purple Thread

SOLVE THE PUZZLE & GET ONE STEP CLOSER TO LEARNING THE SECRET OF THE GOLDEN THREAD

1 2 3 4 | 5 | 6 7 8 9 10 | 11 | 12 13 14 15 | 16 17 18 19 20 | 21 22

23 24 25 26 27 28 | 29 30 31 : " 32 33 34 | 35 36 37 38 | 39 40 41 42 | 43 44 45

46 47 48 49 50 51 52 53 54 | 55 56 57 | 58 59 60 | 61 62 34 63 64 | 65 66 67 | 68 69 70

71 72 73 74 75 76 77 | 78 79 | 80 81 82 | 83 84 85 , | 86 87 88 | 89 90 91

92 93 94 95 96 97 98 99 100 | 101 102 | 103 104 105 | 106 107 108 109 110 111 112 . | 113 114 115 | 116 112 117

118 119 120 121 122 123 124 | 62 79 | 40 125 126 | 127 128 62 129 6 130 131 132 | 133 134 135

136 137 138 139 140 141 142 , | 34 2 101 | 143 144 145 146 147 148 149 | 150 6 151 152 | 153 154 102 84 155 156

96 157 158 | 159 13 160 | 161 162 163 | 164 165 166 | 167 168 169 6 170 , | 6 171 172 | 173 174 175 176

6 177 178 179 180 181 | 182 78 34 183 . | 184 103 185 186 | 187 188 189 190 191 192 59 193 194 | 80 195 196 197

90 198 199 | 200 201 | 202 2 203 | 204 205 53 80 206 | 13 113 | 139 112 207 | 208 209 210 211 | 212 213 214

215 216 | 94 2 217 | 34 17 218 219 | 40 113 | 184 59 220 221 222 | 89 223 224 99 225 226 114 227 163

51 2 228 163 | 181 229 135 | 230 76 99 | 231 40 232 233 | 58 103 234 235 236 | 237 238 239 240 241 | 242 33

243 125 144 6 | 244 245 | 129 13 | 246 2 247 248 249 250 | 102 251 101 252 | 85 253 254 99 2 .

58 112 255 256 257 102 78 258 259 | 260 261 262 13 263 39 264 , | 163 96 121 | 6 265 266 267 268 269 270 | 271 272 88

100 96 81 | 34 90 33 | 181 34 273 274 275 | 276 277 | 139 59 278 41 ! | 279 280 37 281 282 283 94 284 53 285

12 : 10 - 12

The Scarlet Thread

Scrambled word	Letters	Numbers
DOG	3	44 70
DAMA	4	50
EEV	3	35 124
ATNAS	5	68 113 9 77
ICNA	4	140 15 82
NAOH	4	101 6 114
HABRAAM	7	17
RASHA	5	81 42
HAGRA	5	33
SEIHALM	7	108 153 85 13
CISAA	5	54 88 93
CCBEERA	7	2 51 103

Scrambled word	Letters	Numbers
CAJBO	5	94 24
SAEU	4	123 149 3
EHLACR	6	43 57
HAEL	4	58 133 38
DUJHA	5	7 73
VELI	4	89 97 34
HOSJEP	6	45 8 141 137 122
NIJEAMNB	8	59 144 22 56 80 49
DISMEWVI	8	148 78 99 12 129
MIIRAM	6	130 19 131
SOSME	5	100 126 16
RAAHHPO	7	143 119 150 75 29
HEBESWR	7	115 112 26

LEARN THE KEY TO UNDERSTANDING THE SCARLET THREAD AND YOU WILL BE ONE STEP CLOSER TO LEARNING THE SECRET TO THE GOLDEN THREAD

Word	Boxes (number under each box; □ = unnumbered)
NAARO	□ □ 127 107 20
SIVETLE	90 147 46 139 5 □ 86
TOEHRJ	□ 92 53 11 138 111
SIPES	□ □ □ □ 32
SUHJOA	□ 120 67 69 21 □
BACEL	10 145 95 109 □
GESJUD	□ 61 14 118 □ □
LAEMUS	□ 83 116 25 □ 96
ASLU	□ 27 71 105
IDDVA	98 □ 125 66 40
LOOSOMN	□ [illegible] [illegible] □ [illegible] □ [illegible]
NIELAD	102 152 39 117 36 110
HAMREJEI	□ 47 104 60 □ 151 76 87
EARZ	□ □ 48 128
MIENEHHA	4 □ 65 □ □ □ □ 132
RESTEH	□ □ 23 135 □ 134
RENCINBESHA	□ □ 30 52 □ 106 □ 74 □ □ 91
HAEKEHIZ	□ □ □ □ □ 31 □ 55
DAERICOM	□ 1 □ 121 136 146 □ □
NOHJA	□ 18 64 □ □
PPHOERST	□ □ 63 62 79 □ 41 28

The Scarlet Thread

DID YOU FOLLOW THE THREADS?

The Scarlet Thread

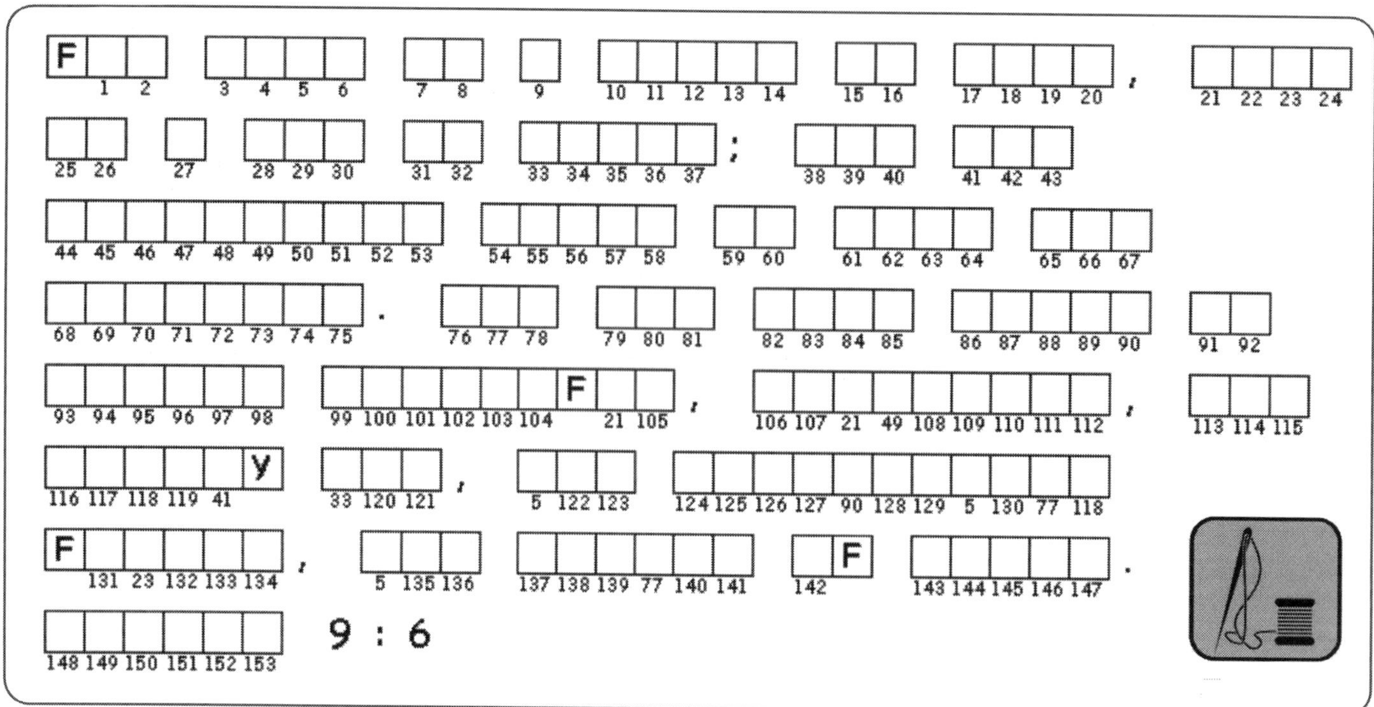

Family Tree Review Puzzle

Across
3. Mother of Samuel
5. Wife of Moses
8. Jacobs favorite son
9. Eldest son of Isaac
11. Mother of Jacob
14. First wife of Jacob
15. Husband of Eve
16. Mother of Ishmael

Down
1. Mother of Solomon
2. Father of Solomon
4. The father of Joseph
6. Son of Hagar
7. Jacobs Father
9. Mother of Abel
10. Father of Abraham
12. Father of Isaac
13. Wife of Abraham

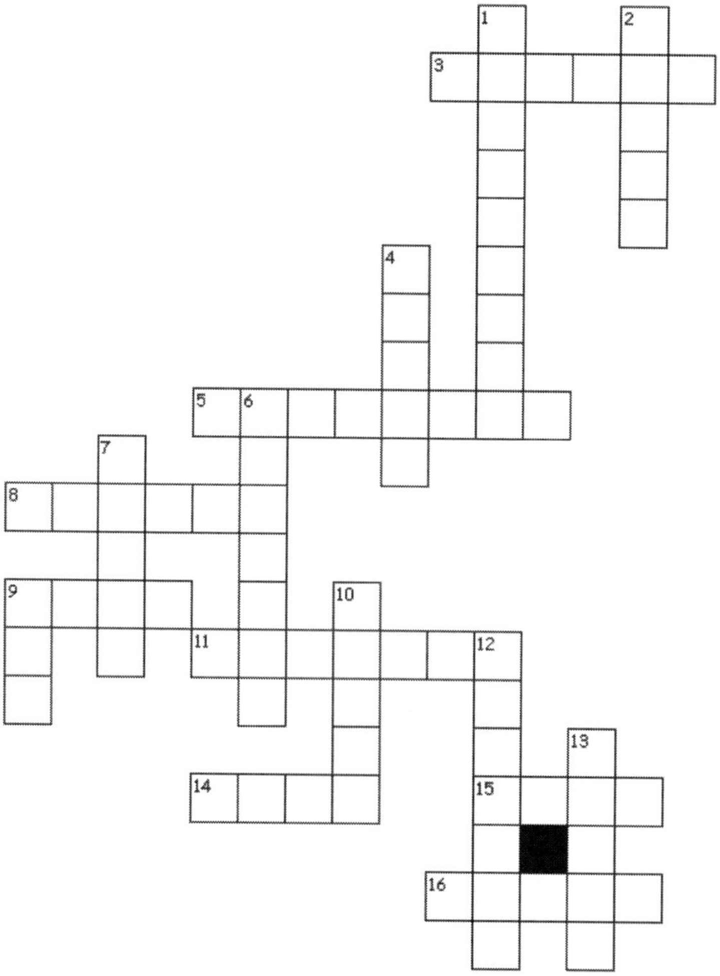

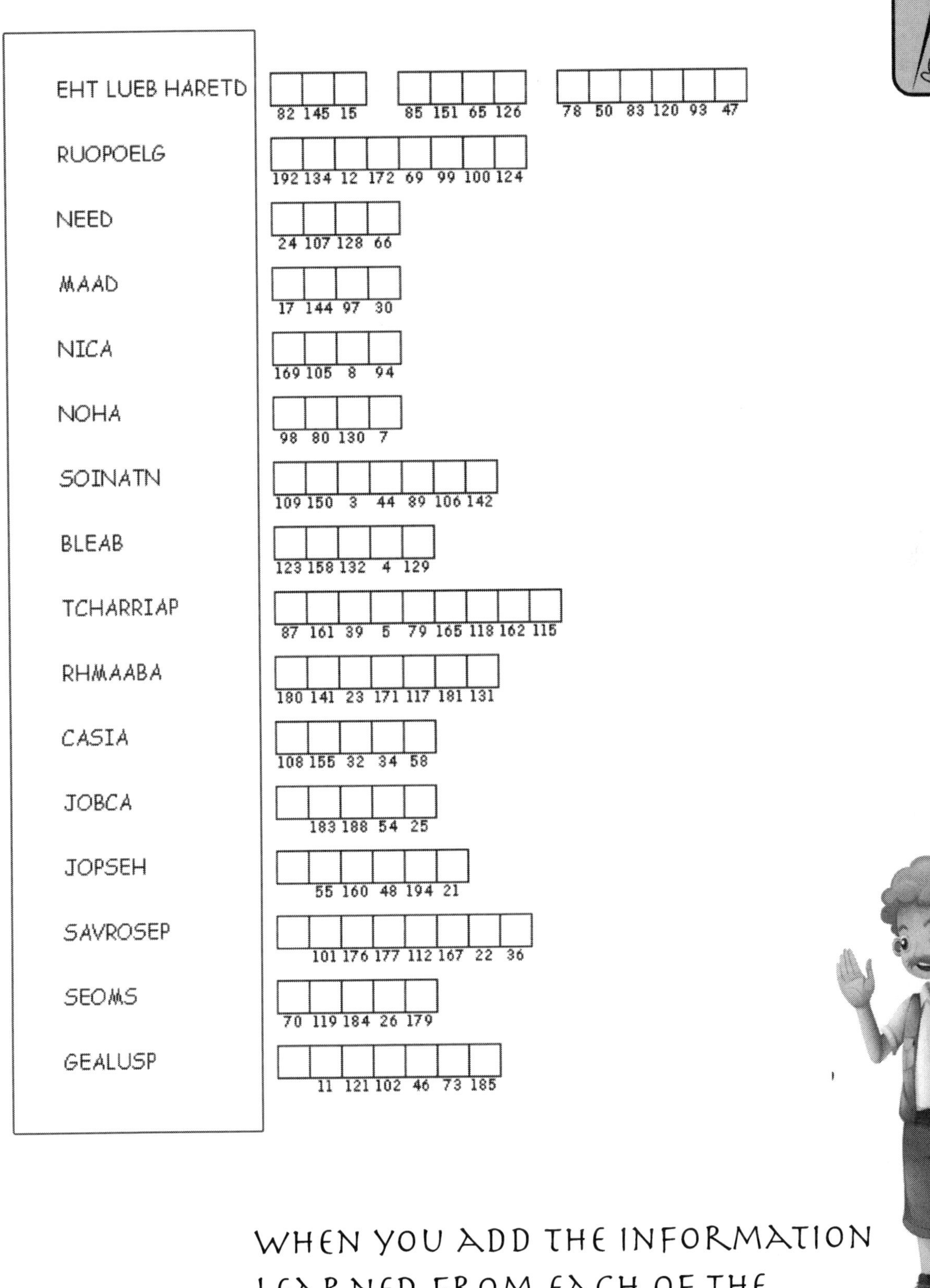

WHEN YOU ADD THE INFORMATION LEARNED FROM EACH OF THE THREADS THEN YOU WILL HAVE ACCESS TO EACH OF THE CLUES

The Blue Thread

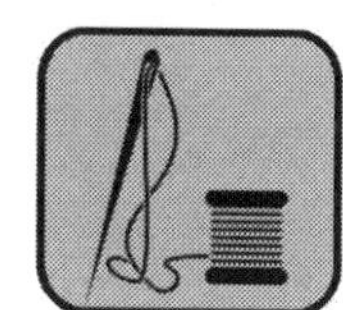

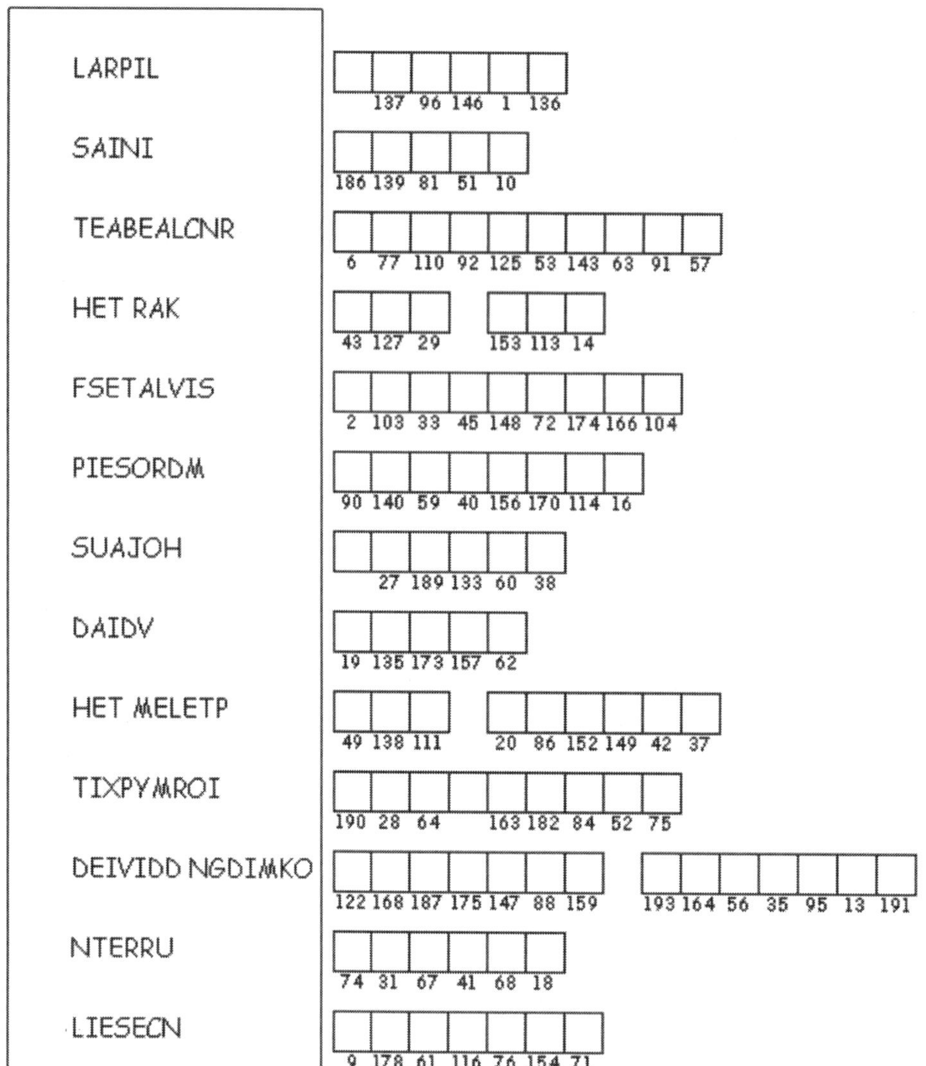

FOLLOW THE THREADS TO DISCOVER THE KEYS THAT WILL REVEAL THE ANSWER TO THE MYSTERY

The Blue Thread

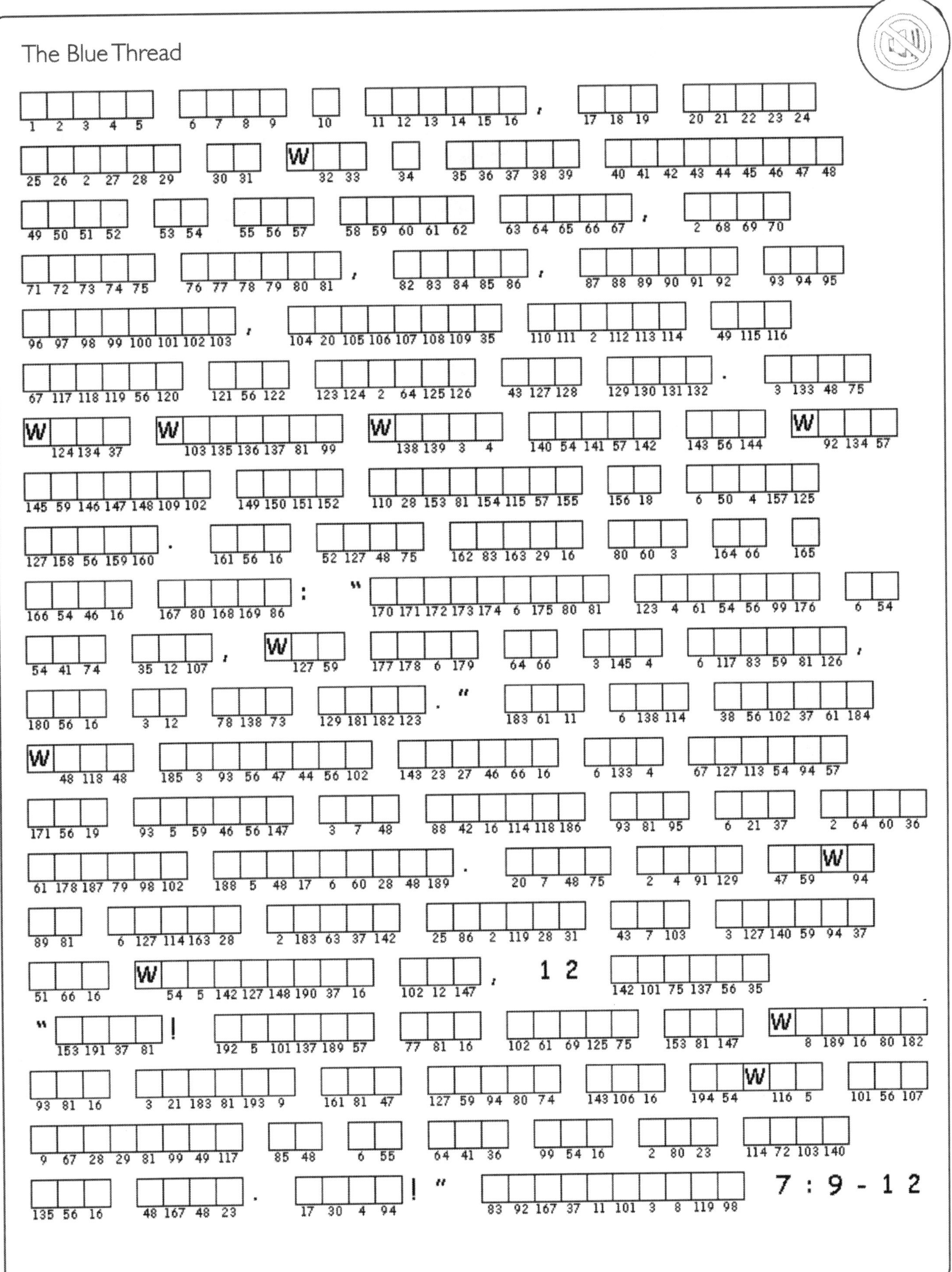

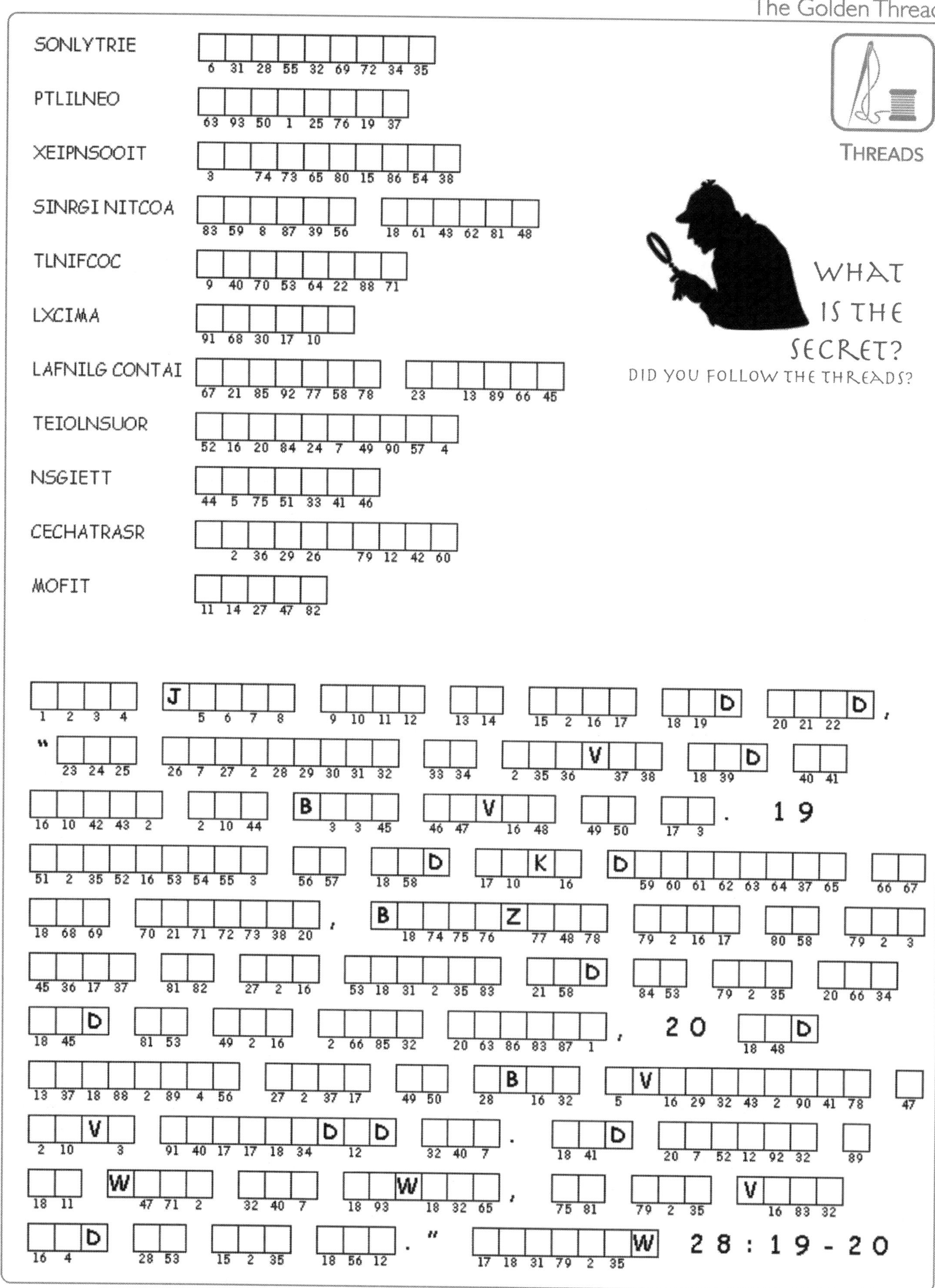
THREADS
SONLYTRIE
PTLILNEO
XEIPNSOOIT
SINRGI NITCOA
TLNIFCOC
LXCIMA
LAFNILG CONTAI
TEIOLNSUOR
NSGIETT
CECHATRASR
MOFIT
WHAT IS THE SECRET?
DID YOU FOLLOW THE THREADS?
19
20
28:19-20

Made in the USA
Columbia, SC
23 June 2022

62103674R00091